More praise for *The Classroom Teacher's Technology Survival Guide*

"With so much written about technology in schools and so little of it that is both practical and thoughtful, *The Classroom Teacher's Technology Survival Guide* splendidly meets those often-ignored standards. Thank you, Doug Johnson."

—**Larry Cuban**, Professor Emeritus of Education, Stanford University

"It is no surprise that *The Classroom Teacher's Technology Survival Guide* reads with the easy-to-understand sage advice of this seasoned veteran. In Garrison Keillor–style comfort, Doug takes the reader on a building spiral of more sophisticated learning, peppered with humorous and down-home bits of wisdom honed from decades of diligence and success. Readers can use the book for personal learning, a book study, or to be more informed as a participant in a school or district technology leadership committee. Experienced or future educational technology directors or CTOs can gather insights in how to work with the educators in their district on their continued journey to maximize effective technology-enhanced strategies, along with some inspiring anecdotes."

—**Gordon K. Dahlby**, PhD, Educational Technology Advisor/Consultant, *Leadership in Policy, Planning and Practice*

"Doug's trademark humor and humility will help any teacher—whether novice or expert—navigate the difficult terrain of classroom technology integration. This is a great resource for a building-wide book study!"

—**Dr. Scott McLeod**, Associate Professor, Educational Leadership, and Founding Director, CASTLE, University of Kentucky

"Let Doug Johnson, an educator's educator, be your guide-on-the-side to make the most effective, most efficient use of technology in your classroom—whatever your grade level, whatever your subject."

—**David Chojnacki**, Executive Director, Near East South Asia Council of Overseas Schools

"Mashing handy checklists, practical wisdom, deep experience, and a refreshingly honest dose of skepticism, Doug Johnson coaches even the most reluctant teachers and administrators to plan a move from basic to meaningful to transformational use of new and emerging technologies."

—**Joyce Kasman Valenza**, PhD, Teacher-Librarian at Springfield (PA) Township HS Library, author, and technology advocate.

"Doug Johnson's latest book, *The Classroom Teacher's Technology Survival Guide*, is required reading for all educators. Appropriate for any experience level, the book is a comprehensive field guide to effective teaching with technology."

—**Ric Wiltse**, Executive Director, Michigan Association for Computer Users in Learning (MACUL)

"Disruptive technologies, productivity tools, cloud computing—the 21st century is rife with acronyms and Gordian knots. Doug Johnson's keen insight cuts through the essence of what classroom teachers—and their principals—need to know to make learning happen."

—**Miguel Guhlin**, Director of Instructional Technology Services for the San Antonio Independent School District and author of the *Around the Corner* blog

Jossey-Bass Teacher

Jossey-Bass Teacher provides educators with practical knowledge and tools to create a positive and lifelong impact on student learning. We offer classroom-tested and research-based teaching resources for a variety of grade levels and subject areas. Whether you are an aspiring, new, or veteran teacher, we want to help you make every teaching day your best.

From ready-to-use classroom activities to the latest teaching framework, our value-packed books provide insightful, practical, and comprehensive materials on the topics that matter most to K–12 teachers. We hope to become your trusted source for the best ideas from the most experienced and respected experts in the field.

Titles in the Jossey-Bass Teacher Survival Guide Series

First-Year Teacher's Survival Guide: Ready-to-Use Strategies, Tools & Activities for Meeting the Challenges of Each School Day, Second Edition ● Julia G. Thompson ● ISBN 978-0-7879-9455-6

The Art Teacher's Survival Guide for Elementary and Middle Schools, Second Edition
Helen D. Hume ● ISBN 978-0-470-18302-1

The Classroom Teacher's Survival Guide: Practical Strategies, Management Techniques and Reproducibles for New and Experienced Teachers, Third Edition
Ronald L. Partin ● ISBN 978-0-470-45364-3

Writing Workshop Survival Kit, Second Edition
Gary Robert Muschla ● ISBN 978-0-7879-7619-4

Special Educator's Survival Guide, Second Edition
Roger Pierangelo, Ph.D. ● ISBN 978-0-7879-7096-3

The English Teacher's Survival Guide: Ready-to-Use Techniques & Materials for Grades 7–12, Second Edition
Mary Lou Brandvik and Katherine S. McKnight ● ISBN 978-0-470-52513-5

School Newspaper Advisers Survival Guide ● Patricia Osborn ● ISBN 978-0-7879-6624-9

Play Director's Survival Kit: A Complete Step-by-Step Guide to Producing Theater in Any School or Communtity Setting
James W. Rodgers and Wanda C. Rodgers ● ISBN 978-0-87628-565-7

Math Teacher's Survival Guide: Practical Strategies, Management Techniques, and Reproducibles for New and Experienced Teachers, Grades 5–12
Judith A. Muschla, Gary Robert Muschla, and Erin Muschla ● ISBN 978-0-470-40764-6

A Survival Kit for the Elementary School Principal: With Reproducible Forms, Checklists & Letters ● Abby Barry Bergman ● ISBN 978-0-7879-6639-3

The Reading Teacher's Survival Kit: Ready-to-Use Checklists, Activities and Materials to Help All Students Become Successful Readers
Wilma H. Miller Ed.D. ● ISBN 978-0-13-042593-5

Biology Teacher's Survival Guide: Tips, Techniques & Materials for Success in the Classroom ● Michael F. Fleming ● ISBN 978-0-13-045051-7

The Elementary/Middle School Counselor's Survival Guide, Third Edition
John J. Schmidt, Ed.D. ● 978-0-470-56085-3

Discipline Survival Guide for the Secondary Teacher, Second Edition
Julia G. Thompson ● ISBN 978-0-470-54743-4

The Substitute Teaching Survival Guide, Grades K–5: Emergency Lesson Plans and Essential Advice ● John Dellinger ● ISBN 978-0-7879-7410-7

The Substitute Teaching Survival Guide, Grades 6–12: Emergency Lesson Plans and Essential Advice ● John Dellinger ● ISBN 978-0-7879-7411-4

The Classroom Teacher's Technology Survival Guide

DOUG JOHNSON

JOSSEY-BASS
A Wiley Imprint
www.josseybass.com

Published by Jossey-Bass
A Wiley Imprint
One Montgomery Street, Suite 1200, San Francisco, CA 94104-4594—www.josseybass.com

Jossey-Bass books and products are available through most bookstores. To contact Jossey-Bass directly call our Customer Care Department within the U.S. at 800-956-7739, outside the U.S. at 317-572-3986, or fax 317-572-4002.

Wiley publishes in a variety of print and electronic formats and by print-on-demand. Some material included with standard print versions of this book may not be included in e-books or in print-on-demand. If this book refers to media such as a CD or DVD that is not included in the version you purchased, you may download this material at http://booksupport.wiley.com. For more information about Wiley products, visit www.wiley.com.

Library of Congress Cataloging-in-Publication Data

Johnson, Doug, 1952-
   The classroom teacher's technology survival guide / Doug Johnson. — 1st ed.
      p. cm. — (The Jossey-Bass teacher survival guide series)
   Includes bibliographical references and index.
   ISBN 978-1-118-02455-3 (pbk.)
 1. Educational technology.   2.   Education—Effect of technological innovations on.   I. Title.
   LB1028.3.J6 2012
   371.33—dc23

                                                              2011039116

Printed in the United States of America
FIRST EDITION

PB Printing   10 9 8 7 6 5 4 3 2 1

This book is dedicated to the caring teachers, librarians, and administrators of the Mankato Area Public Schools who teach me every day.

Special thanks to Anne Hanson, Mary Mehsikomer, Miguel Guhlin, and Blue Skunk readers who offered suggestions for improvement to early drafts of this book.

About the Book

The Classroom Teacher's Technology Survival Guide has been written for educators who want good teaching, not technology, as the focus of their classroom.

Starting with a simple strategy for thinking about the "big picture" of technology use in schools and some basic questions and answers about computers, software, and networking (for example, What type of computer should I have?), the book outlines pragmatic ways all teachers can use computers, the Internet, digital cameras, and other technology tools to enhance their professional productivity.

The book includes dozens of strategies a classroom teacher can use to both enhance current educational practices and create motivating project-based units. Practical advice on creating good project assessments, handling the potential distractions technologies may cause, and dealing with issues of safe and appropriate use provides guidance for teachers at all grade levels. The book concludes with suggestions about how educators can help determine their own "technology future" and suggested resources for further study.

Peppered throughout each chapter are "survival tips" I have discovered in my nearly thirty years of work with teachers and technology in schools. Designed to be readable and realistic, this book can help any educator turn technology into a genuine tool for enhancing teaching and learning.

About the Author

Doug Johnson has been the director of media and technology for the Mankato (Minnesota) Public Schools since 1991 and has served as an adjunct faculty member at Minnesota State University since 1990. His teaching experience includes work in grades K–12, both here and in Saudi Arabia. He is the author of five books: *The Indispensable Librarian, The Indispensable Teacher's Guide to Computer Skills, Teaching Right from Wrong in the Digital Age, Machines Are the Easy Part; People Are the Hard Part,* and *School Libraries Head for the Edge.* His long-running column "Head for the Edge" appears in *Library Media Connection.* Doug's Blue Skunk blog averages over fifty thousand visits a month, and his articles have appeared in over forty books and periodicals. Doug has conducted workshops and given presentations for over 150 organizations throughout the United States as well as in Malaysia, Kenya, Thailand, Germany, Poland, Canada, Chile, Peru, Brazil, Egypt, Jordan, the UAE, and Australia. He has held a variety of leadership positions in state and national organizations, including the International Society for Technology in Education and the American Association of School Librarians.

Contents

Readings and Resources **209**

Index **215**

Introduction

Why This Book?

As a veteran classroom teacher, I always dreaded my administrator going to a conference. Invariably she would return with a new educational "silver bullet" for improving teaching and learning and expect us teachers to implement it. This usually meant a ton of additional work despite our being already very, very busy actually teaching. And unfortunately these new processes, techniques, and plans were abandoned when the next silver bullet rolled around. Yesterday it was "outcomes-based education." Today it is "essential learning outcomes."

A survival strategy that many of us adopted was to keep doing what we'd always been doing but use the vocabulary of the new thing. We'd keep quiet during staff development sessions and quietly pray, "This too shall pass." It was difficult not to become cynical about any change effort in school because we knew there would be another initiative coming before we could finish implementing the first one.

The use of information technologies in schools is a different matter. As we look at society in general, technology has had and continues to have a powerful impact on the way things are being done. No one would think that medical CAT scans, online banking and shopping, or computerized diagnostics of motor vehicles are a "passing fad." And to think that the use of technology in schools is a passing fad doesn't make any sense either.

At the same time, both administrators and teachers are finding they need to work together to meet the ambitious objective of reaching *all* students. Change must be meaningful, effective, and practical. The only way to achieve this kind of change is through teacher-principal teamwork on common goals.

Classroom teachers have a finite amount of energy and time to devote to change. So why not invest in the kinds of changes that will be with us not until the next silver bullet comes along but for the remainder of our careers? Why not consider making changes that consistently benefit our students? Although technology does change—sometimes at what seems to be an impossibly fast pace—the basics of its use in education have been and will be with us for many years.

This book is about the basic use of technology in the classroom. It's written for teachers who do not consider themselves technology enthusiasts but who still want to harness the power of the tools and strategies that can truly improve their instruction and the learning experience of their students.

If you are a teacher who wants the benefits of using technology but who also wants to lead a normal life away from a keyboard and monitor, read on.

Why Is an English Teacher Writing This Book Instead of Bill Gates?

My approach to technology perhaps can be explained by the circumstances under which I started using it. As a half-time librarian and half-time English teacher in a small junior high school, I found an Apple II computer sitting on my desk at the beginning of the 1982 school year. Yes, dear readers, I *am* older than dirt. I was pretty darned mad that (1) somebody had decided the school needed a computer in the first place, (2) the library budget was used to buy it, and (3) I was supposed to be the one to figure out the dumb hunk of plastic.

After three rather frustrating days, I produced my first half-page memo using Apple Writer, a daisy-wheel printer, and more patience than I ever thought I could muster. But by the time I finished the memo, I was deeply in love with the little machine.

The Apple II and its word processing program, both primitive by today's standards, were a writer's dream. They compensated for my bad spelling and handwriting. I could revise without retyping an entire document. My printed documents looked professional. My students could read rather than decode my tests and worksheets.

Then a little lightbulb appeared over my head. "I teach seventy-five kids every day who struggle with their writing as well. If this thing helps me, just think what it might do for them!" I couldn't wait to share my enthusiasm with my seventh graders and fellow teachers.

Over the past thirty years, I've fallen in love quite a number of times with these silicon-enhanced creatures. I am enamored yet of how productive spreadsheets, databases, and multimedia presentation programs have made me. It's tough to imagine having to be separated from e-mail or the information resources of the Web even temporarily. My smartphone goes everywhere with me. I spend an increasing amount of time learning from distant fellow professionals through social networking tools: blogs, wikis, Facebook, and webinars.

This is not to say that these relationships have always been easy. I am not, by nature, a techie. Even the remote controls in the family room exacerbate my

IDS (Intelligence Deficit Syndrome). In schools, I've watched teachers spend too much time trying to learn poorly designed technologies and use technology for entertainment rather than real engagement. I shudder when schools take a "ready, fire, aim" approach to technology planning by buying often-expensive gizmos and then running about looking for problems those gizmos might solve. Even more frustrating is when schools buy expensive gizmos and don't provide teachers with adequate training in how to use them—that is, in both how to operate them and how to employ them as tools to deliver instruction. I worry that monies spent on technology in schools might be taken from the budgets of other programs that might have greater value to kids.

My love of technology is conditional, and that is what this book reflects. You will find my ideas informed, practical, and perhaps even a little skeptical. But most of all I hope you find the ideas in this book useful when seeking ways to benefit your students with the judicious use of technology.

I'd be delighted if you were to e-mail me about anything I write in this book at dougj@doug-johnson.com. I look forward to reading *your* ideas.

Creating the Essential Conditions Needed for Successful Technology Use

A lack of support is a primary reason why teachers haven't more rapidly adopted technology. The list in the sample letter that follows summarizes essential conditions that teachers need if they are to truly integrate technology into their classroom in meaningful ways.

Dear School Leader . . .

Dear School Leader:

Let's work together to create an environment that will help maximize my success when working with technology in the classroom. These conditions will help me a lot and show that technology integration is something you care about.

❑ **1. Make teaching students technology skills a district priority.** Until the high-stakes tests and state standards require that I teach technology skills, I must focus my teaching efforts on what *is* tested and mandated. Our school board goals are all about reading, writing, and math. Until you tell me technology skills are important for my students to master, I can't spend a week in a computer lab teaching something such as writing a complex sentence or designing a chart that I can teach in a day with paper and pencil.

❑ **2. Show me research demonstrating that using technology is more effective than traditional methods.** Until there is unbiased research that shows I can teach basic and content-area skills using technology more effectively than I can using traditional methods, I am reluctant to change how I teach. After all, I do a pretty good job now. Unless research indicates that spending money on technology will help me do a better job, I feel I need to continue to advocate for school budgets that spend more on smaller class sizes; library, art, and music programs; and services for students with special needs.

❑ **3. Provide technology in my school that is reliable, adequate, and secure.** I use the telephone, the overhead projector, and the VCR in my classroom because I can count on them working. I'm reluctant to use computers, LCD projectors, interactive whiteboards, the Internet, and any other new devices unless they work 99 percent of the time. If you ask me to create separate lesson plans for when the technology works and when it doesn't, I will suspect you were never a classroom teacher yourself. If I have thirty children in my class, please provide thirty computers that actually work in the lab or on a laptop cart. Help me find ways to reduce my worries about online stranger danger and inappropriate Web sites.

❑ **4. Show me that technology use is safe and developmentally appropriate.** Science just hasn't shown the impact on small human beings of staring at computer screens or using keyboards. We do know childhood obesity is on the rise because too many children are inactive. Please let me know when playing with blocks on the screen is proven to be as developmentally beneficial as playing with blocks on the floor.

❑ **5. Hire or develop technology support people with interpersonal skills.** You know that I am neither a child nor an idiot. I don't like it when techs treat me like one. Please provide me with technology instructors who let me run my own mouse when learning even if it takes a little longer, who use layman's English when explaining, and who tell me only what I need to know. Cut out the cute asides like calling a problem an SUD (Stupid User Dysfunction). I know what such acronyms mean. I also need timely technical support. If I have to wait three days to get my computer working again, can you blame me for developing a negative attitude about using it?

❏ **6. Ensure that all technology comes with effective training.** Classes about a technology that I *might* someday need—taught by an instructor who hasn't been near a school lately—too often feel like a waste of my time. Teach me in a small group about the things I need to do *today* to be effective. And how about a little follow-up? Please give me time to connect with my peers about what we have learned, what's working, and what isn't. We are finding professional learning communities effective in implementing other kinds of pedagogical change.

❏ **7. Support technology that is genuinely time-saving.** Please don't ask me to learn how to use a technology to make someone else's job easier—like the technology department's or the administration's. I don't have time to log into my computer on three separate screens to get to an application, especially when the required usernames and passwords are long and impossible to remember. I really do understand the importance of security, but it needs to be balanced with convenience.

❏ **8. Most of all, please remember that, as a teacher, I consider myself first a child advocate, second an educator, and only third a technology user.** We'll make a great team if you think of yourself in those terms as well.

Sincerely,
Norm L. Teacher

CHAPTER ONE

Why Should Classroom Teachers Be Technologically Skillful?

U.S. schools spend billions of dollars on educational technology each year. While education budgets shrink, classroom sizes grow, accountability measures skyrocket, and teacher salaries remain stagnant, one has to wonder if this huge investment in wires, motherboards, and things that go beep in the night is actually improving schools' effectiveness.

I don't know that anyone has the definitive answer. It depends on whom you ask, what is being measured, and how educational "effectiveness" is defined. There is a good deal of research out there, little of it conclusive and much of it sponsored by those who have a financial interest in its outcome. Critical writings abound, including the Alliance for Childhood's *Fool's Gold* report (2000); Jane Healey's book *Failure to Connect* (1999); and Larry Cuban's book *Oversold and Underused: Computers in the Classroom* (2003). Admittedly, these references are a bit dated, but they raise valid arguments in terms of the monetary investment in educational technology versus the lack of evidence-based research on the outcomes.

What's a classroom teacher to think? Are personal investment in technology and the hours it takes to learn about it worthwhile? One may not have a choice.

In her book *In the Age of the Smart Machine* from way back in 1989, professor Shoshana Zuboff presciently described two distinct types of impact technology has on the workplace: *automating* and *informating*. The first thing businesses do is automate with information technologies, taking standard operations and making them faster, more accurate, and less labor intensive. But the real power of technology, Zuboff argues, is evident when it starts allowing organizations and individuals to do things that would not be possible without it.

Confused? Let's look at some examples from education:

- Electronic grade books *automate* the functions of the good old red booklets, allowing grades to be calculated, class lists imported, and grades exported to the student information system. But when the grade book is made Web-accessible to parents, they can monitor their children's progress in real time and intervene long before the conference at the end of the first grading period. Some systems even e-mail parents when their child receives a failing grade on a test. That's *informating*.

- Moving worksheets and tutorials onto the computer screen *automates* drill and practice teaching, enhancing it with immediate feedback and engaging sounds and visuals. In *informated* programs the tests and tutorials serve as a means of formative testing, giving the teacher the knowledge of precisely which skills individual students need to learn (ideally before the next big state test).

- The traditional "stand and deliver" lecture that is common in so many classrooms can be *automated* by enhancing it with a well-designed presentation that might include clarifying photographs, diagrams, and highlighted key concepts. Multimedia production tools *informate* the educational process when students themselves use them to communicate the results of constructivist-based learning activities that require higher-level thinking skills and original solutions to problems.

- Computers in labs, libraries, and classrooms *automate* the standard educational practices of writing, computation, and research. Small communication devices wirelessly connected to networks, such as laptops and handheld computers, *informate* the learning environment, allowing their student users anytime, anyplace access to resources, learning opportunities, experts, and each other. These devices have the potential of providing individualized instructional programs to every child, not just those identified as having special needs. Aren't we all, to some extent, learners with "special needs"?

Just as technology has reshaped the business sector over the last two decades, it is reshaping the educational landscape in powerful ways and will continue to do so at an accelerated pace.

Revolution or Evolution in Educational Change?

Easy to do is easy to say.

Attitude plays a major part in any change effort. (I know, "Well, duh!") Geoffrey Moore, in his book *Inside the Tornado* (2004), neatly divides people implementing new technologies into visionaries and pragmatists, and suggests we need to work with each group differently (p. 18):

Visionaries	Pragmatists
Intuitive	Analytic
Support revolution	Support evolution
Contrarian	Conformist
Break away from the pack	Stay with the herd
Follow their own dictates	Consult with colleagues
Take risks	Manage risks
Motivated by future opportunities	Motivated by present problems
Seek what is possible	Pursue what is probable

After years of living in denial, I must come clean. I am a *pragmatist*. Perhaps I was once a visionary, but having worked with real people, contended with real technologies, and been employed by real schools for the past thirty years, I am now a full-fledged pragmatist.

Survival tip: As a former classroom teacher and librarian and as a current technology director, I understand the apprehension about technology felt by many competent, effective, and thoughtful teachers. For those who are reluctant, I offer this advice:

1. Invest time in learning computing basics.

2. Use what technologies personally empower you with your students. If a word processor makes you a better writer, use that technology with your students. If a graphing program helps you better visualize math concepts, share it with your classes. If you enjoy networking with your peers online, communicate with your students and their families who also enjoy using such methods.

3. Become a colearner with your students in regard to technology. Kids will always be more knowledgeable and comfortable with the gizmos than us "mature" folks. Let them teach you or join them in learning something new.

4. Be skeptical, but remain open-minded. Unless the new technology has sufficient potential for learning opportunities for your students, don't jump in. These bright toys can be fun and seductive. Just make sure they have a purpose.

5. Expect reliable, secure, and adequate resources from your school. You shouldn't need to create two sets of lessons plans: one for when the technology works and one for when it doesn't.

And instead of being ashamed, I am proud. Sure, it's exciting to hear those pointy-heads pontificate about how things "really ought to be," but putting vision into practice is where we pragmatists shine—where the vision is practical, of course. And when it actually makes sense for our students and for us.

Of course the chance of success must be high. The change must be demonstrated in other schools to have actually improved kids' or teachers' lives. I would argue that making something work in the real world on a broad scale takes as much genius as, or greater genius than, thinking it up in the first place.

A visionary pundit might describe how using "tags" within a social bookmarking site can facilitate the collaborative problem-solving process. Visionary! Very cool! But when I demonstrated social bookmarking to a group of teachers, one excitedly raised her hand and asked, "Do you mean students could store their research paper bookmarks there so they could keep them even after the tech director reimages the lab? Or could get to them from any computer?" Pragmatic! Very cool! Bless her big, practical heart.

Let's hold our heads high, fellow pragmatists. We're doing good things. It just takes us a little longer.

Developing a Framework for Thinking About Technology in Schools

Ever had these thoughts?

- If the technology worked all the time and like it was supposed to, I'd use it.
- Those technicians! They have the computers so locked up, the kids can't do anything.
- Seems like we are always short of powerful computers for students, but the folks at the district office always have new machines.
- Another grade book program to learn! Why can't the district just pick one and stay with it?
- We're putting students' records online? How do I know they will be secure?
- I'd like to do more project-based units, but it seems the resources just aren't there.
- What do kids really need to know about and be able to do with computers?

Such statements often stem from a lack of a holistic view of technology use in schools—on the part of both teachers and administrators. The magazines teachers read stress the classroom uses of technology. The conferences educators attend often are filled with vendors who are trying to sell packages for managing instruction, software solutions, or devices that are only small pieces of the educational technology use puzzle. Staff development efforts focus on learning how to use management software without helping teachers understand how their efforts fit into their school's overall goals. Why does this occur?

Too few educators have a "big picture" understanding of educational technology use—of technology planning and implementation in terms of hierarchical needs. All who are affected by the educational uses of technology need to understand the overall dimensions of its use if they are to accept it. What follows is a planning model that is comprehensive and simple enough for all educational stakeholders to understand.

Remember Maslow from your college education foundations classes back in the last century?

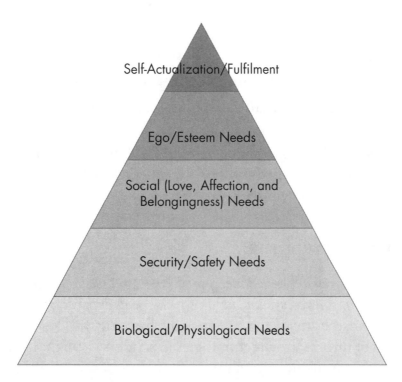

An Interpretation of Maslow's Hierarchy of Needs

In simple terms, Maslow's theory states that before one can have the important things in life, such as love, self-esteem, or fulfillment, some basic needs, such as food and safety, must be satisfied.

We can extend Maslow's theory to the implementation of technology in schools as well. I have called this new theory Johnson's Hierarchy of Educational Technology Needs. Much as Maslow theorizes that physiological needs come before psychological needs, a school district must meet its infrastructure needs before it can reach its goal of using technology to empower learners.

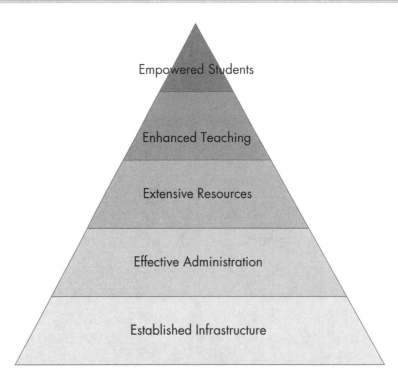

Johnson's Hierarchy of Educational Technology Needs

The following paragraphs describe each of the "needs" in the diagram; how it influences student performance; and how, if not met, it keeps you, the classroom teacher, from being able to help students learn.

ESTABLISHED INFRASTRUCTURE

The district must have a reliable, adequate, cost-effective, and secure technology infrastructure that supports the learning, teaching, and administrative goals of the district.

One of the most critical and potentially limiting factors in the successful implementation of information technologies in schools is reliability. Nothing keeps an administrator from using a data-mining tool, a librarian from using an online database, a teacher from using a Web-based lesson plan, or a student from creating a multimedia presentation like the uncertainty that the technology might fail at a critical moment. We rely on electricity, natural gas, television, and telephone services because these technologies have reached "five nines" reliability. We can count on them to work 99.999 percent of the time. Although techno-advocates often ask users to have a backup plan in case of technology failure, users have been reluctant to take this precaution. Why? It effectively doubles one's workload.

Adequacy is a second important criterion that must be acquired before users in schools will trust technology for the completion of critical tasks. Administrators will not use online accounting systems if there is a long delay in accessing the program because the available bandwidth is not adequate. Teachers and librarians will not plan units that call for the use of electronic sources of information if there are too few computers for students to use or if they know the computers will be out of commission for testing for several weeks out of the year. Students who cannot rely on working technologies because technicians are overloaded with work will find other means to complete assignments.

Finally, concerns about security keep many users from trusting and using technologies in school. Good data backup practices, enforceable (and enforced) data privacy policies, and hardware and software that prevent unauthorized internal and external access to data on school networks are critical needs for all organizations. A lack of IT professional expertise in many school districts has caused this need to not be met. Educators and parents are skeptical of the extensive use of digital record keeping if they cannot be assured that confidential information about their children will remain confidential.

As a teacher, use this checklist to determine how your district is meeting the need for an established, reliable infrastructure:

❑ **1.** Adequate and reliable Internet access throughout the district

❑ **2.** Adequate and reliable Internet access in all buildings

❑ **3.** Adequate and reliable Internet access in all classrooms, media centers, and labs

❑ **4.** Adequate and reliable wireless network access

❑ **5.** Written IT security and disaster recovery plan

❑ **6.** Firewall security for networks

❑ **7.** User verification through log-in requirements and activity logging

❑ **8.** Districtwide virus protection software

❑ **9.** Districtwide spam (junk e-mail) filtering software

❑ **10.** Districtwide Internet filtering software

❑ **11.** Remote computer desktop monitoring and maintenance

❑ **12.** Backup plan for all data

❑ **13.** Adequate workstations for staff and student use

❑ **14.** Adequate peripheral technologies (printers, scanners, projectors, cameras) for staff and student use

❑ **15.** Adequate and efficient maintenance, repair, and replacement procedures, and availability of an online help desk

❑ **16.** Adequate and reliable telephone access to all classrooms and offices

❑ **17.** Adequate and reliable interactive video access in schools offering distance education classes

❑ **18.** Written and thorough technology use policies

❑ **19.** Adequate leadership and management related to technology planning, budgeting, and policymaking

EFFECTIVE ADMINISTRATION

The district must use technology to improve its administrative effectiveness through efficient business practices, communication, planning, and record keeping.

Schools are also businesses. They must have good accounting, budgeting, and purchasing practices if they are to have credibility with the taxpaying public. They must maintain records of test scores, grades, and attendance of students for state, local, and parental reporting. They must keep personnel records and meet payroll. They must track and control transportation, food service, and special education spending. And all of these needs must be met before teachers can teach and students can learn.

Increased demands for accountability by the public in regard to both expenditures and student achievement have also increased the need for more accurate and sophisticated uses of administrative technology in schools. Efforts to tie measurable student achievement to specific educational practices and their funding will mean that educational decision makers need to gather, organize, store, extract, and analyze data in powerful ways. Effective, efficient data-mining practices are possible only with information technology and educators trained in its use.

Efforts to give educational consumers (parents) the ability to compare schools have resulted in K–12 schools' competing for students. This competition has led to a new emphasis on using technology as a communication tool. Such communication technologies as e-mail, electronic mailing lists, Web sites, and social networks are playing an increasingly important role in how schools both inform parents and the public and receive feedback from them. Schools need to see information technologies as marketing tools and use them as such. Parental access to real-time data about their children's daily performance through Web-accessible grade books and attendance records, teacher Web pages, and curriculum outlines and outcomes, as well as student achievement data showing comparisons among local schools, is as critical for schools to provide as online banking services are now for financial institutions who wish to remain competitive.

It is not just student learning that will suffer as a result of inattention to the administrative uses of technology—the existence of individual schools themselves may hang in the balance.

As a teacher, use this checklist to determine how your district is meeting the school's administrative needs:

☐ **1.** Student information system that can be accessed by administration, and that includes attendance, grading, discipline, health, and scheduling modules and that shares data efficiently with other systems

☐ **2.** Student information system that can be accessed by teaching staff

☐ **3.** Student information system that can be accessed by parents

☐ **4.** Student information system that can be accessed by students

☐ **5.** System that allows data warehousing and data-driven decision making

☐ **6.** Systems specific to the management of finance, transportation, personnel and payroll, lunch programs, special education, building systems, and security

☐ **7.** System for curriculum management

❑ **8.** Portable communication devices for staff use, such as cell phones, laptop computers, tablets, or personal digital assistants (PDAs)

❑ **9.** Online (Web-based) district information

❑ **10.** Online (Web-based) building information

❑ **11.** Online (Web-based) department and classroom information

❑ **12.** Interactive communication tools for the administration (instant messaging, electronic mailing lists, collaborative project tools, shared calendars, and e-mail directories)

❑ **13.** Electronic means of communication with school staff by parents, students, and the community

❑ **14.** Established technology competencies and training opportunities for the school's administration and office staff

❑ **15.** Adopted policies and written guidelines on Internet use, safety, plagiarism, selection and reconsideration of digital resources, copyright, and so on

❑ **16.** Familiarity with policy and ethical practices concerning technology use by administration and office staff

---

Note that both of these lower levels (infrastructure and administrative use) of technology planning do not directly involve student use. But they both have an impact on learning because the needs at these levels must be met in order for the higher-level needs of students to be met. Schools that use technologies to increase administrative efficiency can spend more money on direct instruction, purchase better resources, lower class sizes, and have a better-trained staff. These basic uses of technology support any form of instructional practice, from traditional to constructivist.

EXTENSIVE RESOURCES

Technology must be used to provide the most current, accurate, and extensive information resources possible to all learners in the district and community in a cost-effective and reliable manner and at maximum convenience to the user.

Progressive thinkers in both education and business recognize that acquiring basic skills and memorizing a core of facts, although important, are only the foundation of an education in the twenty-first century. Working collaboratively, recognizing and solving genuine problems, evaluating and using information from both primary and secondary sources, communicating effectively, and assessing one's own performance are the new "basic skills" for workers in an information-based economy.

Many teachers are reluctant to implement a project-based, constructivist approach to learning because of the lack of resources their students can use. Ironically, budget makers often question why technology expenditures are necessary when *our* teachers just use textbooks as the primary information source for instruction. This is a genuine catch-22.

If teachers are to design curriculum materials, instructional units, student activities, and assessment tools that teach 21st-century skills, they will need more extensive information resources than in the past. Information in both print formats (made more accessible through electronic library catalogs and periodical databases) and digital formats, such as online subject area databases, full-text periodical databases, e-books, and reference tools, is necessary if students are to have the learning experiences that lead to the ability to access, process, and communicate information. Information processing and communication tools are also necessary: word processing programs, desktop publishing software, spreadsheets, databases, visual organization tools, Web creation software, graphic creation tools, and digital photograph and video editing tools.

Teachers need access to professional resources that will help them improve their own practice as well. Research databases, electronic journals, electronic mailing lists devoted to professional practice, Web-based professional learning communities, and online classes and tutorials are effective components of any staff development effort.

I would include in this category the need for school library media specialists and technology integration specialists who use their expertise to help both teachers and students use electronic resources meaningfully. Too often human resources are not seen as integral to the successful implementation of technology.

As a teacher, use this checklist to determine how your district is meeting your digital resource needs:

❏ **1.** Sufficient access to computing devices for students to complete assigned work

❑ **2.** Access to a professional library media specialist with skills in selecting, evaluating, and using electronic information sources

❑ **3.** Internet access with minimal filtering

❑ **4.** Access to the online building library catalog

❑ **5.** Access to the online district union library catalog

❑ **6.** Access to online catalogs of public, regional, and academic libraries

❑ **7.** Access to adequate online periodical databases

❑ **8.** Access to adequate online subject-specific databases

❑ **9.** Access to adequate online reference materials including encyclopedias and e-books

❑ **10.** Access to adequate digital image, sound, and video resources

❑ **11.** Access to curriculum and teacher support materials

❑ **12.** Access to a wide variety of computerized productivity programs appropriate to student abilities

❑ **13.** Access to a wide range of educational interactive applications including practices, simulations, and tutorials to support content-area learning objectives

❑ **14.** Access to needed content-specific hardware, such as scientific measurement devices, calculators, and other technology-based education tools

❑ **15.** Access to educational television programming through broadcast and cable television and Internet streaming

❑ **16.** Access to desktop videoconferencing hardware and software

❑ **17.** Software and network resources needed to electronically publish and share school-, teacher-, and student-produced information

ENHANCED TEACHING

All district teachers must have the technology training, skills, and resources needed to ensure that students will meet local and state learning objectives, and they must have the technological means to assess and record student progress.

The meaningful use of information technologies by teachers falls into two categories: *personally productive* and *transformational*. Remember Zuboff's automating and informing from the beginning of this chapter?

Teachers in the *personally productive* mode design more worksheets, guides, and objective tests that are easy to read—all of which are readily modified using a word processor. They more quickly report student grades and attendance using a networked administrative system. They communicate more effectively with students, other staff members, and parents if they can use e-mail and create Web pages. They can access a myriad of already existing learning activities through online repositories. No educational practices genuinely change with these kinds of uses, but traditional tasks can be done more efficiently, effectively, and accurately. When a teacher spends less time creating instructional materials, recording and reporting student progress, and communicating with parents, the time saved can be used for directly interacting with students or for designing more effective lessons or units.

The *transformational* use of technology changes the role of the teacher as well as what is taught and how it is taught. The technology is used to actually restructure the educational process to allow it to do things it has never been able to do before. Such technology use helps teachers do the following:

- Provide instruction that enables all students to master the basic skills of writing, reading, and computation by using a variety of teaching strategies and tools to meet diverse student learning styles

- Design and implement constructivist-based units that provide students with instruction and practice in authentic information literacy and research skills and the higher-order thinking skills inherent in those processes

- Design student performance assessments that lead to improved learning

- Use assistive and adaptive technologies with students with special needs

- Provide students and parents with
  - Individual education plans for every student
  - Continuous feedback on how well students are meeting their learning goals
  - Opportunities for virtual assessments of student performance

- Locate and use research findings that will guide their educational practices

- Collect and interpret data that measure the effectiveness of educational practices

Society is asking schools to accomplish two difficult goals: (1) guarantee that every student has basic skills, and (2) prepare an ever larger number of graduates for a knowledge-based economy that requires workers who are self-motivated, can solve genuine problems, can communicate well, have the interpersonal skills to work collaboratively, and can upgrade their skills by purposely continuing to learn. (See the "Gone Missing" sidebar.) Employing teachers who are well versed in technology use is the only way schools will be able to achieve these results.

As a teacher, use this checklist to determine how your district is meeting your staff development needs:

❑ **1.** Basic professional productivity skills for all teaching staff

❑ **2.** Basic Internet skills for all teaching staff

❑ **3.** Skills related to integrating the use of technology into classroom units for all teaching staff

❑ **4.** Familiarity with policy and ethical practices concerning technology use by teaching staff

❑ **5.** Knowledge of and practice in using adaptive devices with children with special needs

❑ **6.** Assessments to measure the status of teaching staff competencies in technology

❑ **7.** Formal training opportunities for developing technology skills

❑ **8.** Just-in-time training opportunities for developing technology skills

❑ **9.** Ongoing mentoring, troubleshooting, and assistance for staff members when they are developing technology skills

❑ **10.** Technology skill evaluations as a part of teacher evaluations

❑ **11.** Technology skill assessment as a part of the hiring process

❑ **12.** Training in electronic grade book use

❑ **13.** Training in curriculum system and student data-mining program use

❑ **14.** Training in student information system use for reporting grades and attendance reporting

❑ **15.** Training in creating online information for parents, students, and the community

❑ **16.** Training in creating distance learning opportunities (Web based, interactive television, or both) for teachers

❑ **17.** Available information about best practices in regard to the use of technology in the classroom

❑ **18.** Available information about new and emerging technologies and their educational applications

Again note that this lower level of technology use does not directly involve student use of technology. But it has a considerable impact on learning. Teachers who skillfully use technologies can improve traditional methods of instruction and model effective technology use for their students. Constructivist, problem-based units can certainly be designed that do not need technology, but such units can be greatly enhanced by its use.

EMPOWERED STUDENTS

All students will demonstrate the mastered use of technology to access, process, organize, communicate, and evaluate information in order to answer questions and solve problems.

When the basic needs of infrastructure, administration, resources, and teacher understanding are met, schools can provide students with successful technology-enhanced learning opportunities. Student use of technology can be viewed in a hierarchical arrangement as well:

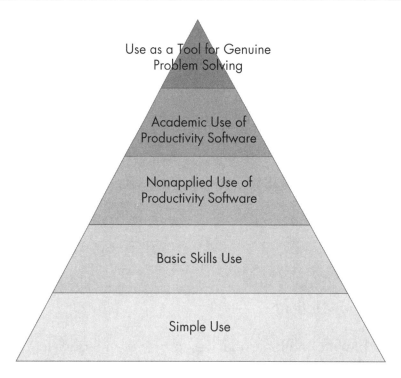

Johnson's Hierarchy of Student Technology Use

Simple Use of Technology

Drill and practice software, integrated learning systems, computer-animated picture books, trivia recall games, and low-level problem-solving and simulation computer software have long been the mainstays of student technology use in most schools. These simple uses are also where a good deal of effort has gone in assessing the effectiveness of "educational computing," which has yielded poor, limited, or mixed results. The use of technology to teach basic skills, memorized facts, or low-level thinking skills, although at times motivational for students, is very expensive for the results achieved. The assessment of this use of technology really has to be an assessment of total student gain of basic skills, which is extremely difficult to determine for many reasons—the Hawthorne effect (results that occur simply because a topic is being studied), the bias of software producers who may be conducting the evaluations, a lack of resources for controlled study groups, and so on. Unfortunately, this technology use currently seems to be tainting decision makers' attitudes concerning all uses of technology in schools. And the actual computer skills students need to use these products are very limited: using a mouse to point and click.

Operational Skills Use of Technology

The second level of technology use is operational. Knowing how to turn on a computer or other piece of equipment, and being able to save files, to print, to adjust desktop settings, and to add or remove software, are skills necessary for most independent computer users. In a school setting, however, many of these activities are restricted or at least discouraged. Management tools are designed to direct students straight to the applications they need without the distractions and possible damage to the operating system.

Nonapplied Use of Technology

Separate classes in "computer literacy" teach students at all grade levels how to use productivity software, such as word processors, databases, spreadsheets, presentation programs, multimedia authoring tools, e-mail, video production equipment, digital reference materials, electronic databases, and network search engines. Although all students should acquire such skills, these skills are somewhat meaningless and soon forgotten if they are not applied to a purpose.

Academic Use of Technology

Increasingly teachers are giving traditional assignments a technology "upgrade." Traditional tasks are completed using technology, and technology adds benefits to those tasks. Although a teacher's upgrading of traditional assignments with the judicious use of technology helps students apply computer skills and improves traditional instructional practices, it still does not tap into technology's potential to serve as a catalyst for pedagogical change, nor does such a scattershot approach guarantee that all students, regardless of teacher or program, will gain identified technology competencies.

Use of Technology as a Tool for Genuine Problem Solving

When students use technology as a tool for completing complex, authentic projects that ask them to solve genuine problems and answer real questions, technology reaches its most powerful instructional potential. This type of use requires students to complete tasks similar to those they will be asked to undertake in information-economy jobs—the kind of work that is better paying and gives greater job satisfaction and that will be the core of our economy both now and in the future.

But big challenges present themselves when technology is used on a large scale as an information processing tool. First, it requires a large investment of time and effort on the part of teachers in learning how to use it. Anybody can learn to operate drill and practice software in a few minutes, but learning to use a database to store, categorize, and sort information can literally take hours of instruction, weeks of practice, genuine effort, and guaranteed episodes of pure frustration. Teachers must spend additional time developing not only lessons that incorporate the computer skill into their specific subject areas but also units that have meaning for students, stress real-world applicability, and require higher-level thinking skills.

Second, the product of such instruction is not a neatly quantifiable indicator on an objective, nationally normed, quickly scored test. Conducting and assessing such projects require the ability to develop and apply standards; delay for long periods of time the satisfaction of task completion; and acknowledge and accept that conclusions, evaluations, and meanings that result from one's efforts are often ambiguous. It means that teachers have to see evaluation as a growth process, not a sorting process.

And finally, students need more than the twenty to forty minutes of lab access per week to learn these uses of technology. That means more equipment and software in more locations than if computers are used simply for accessing electronic worksheets or flash cards—or, increasingly, that means providing every child with a computing device.

Assessment of this technology use needs to be done less to satisfy a state department, legislature, or academic body than to inform the students themselves, their parents, and the community in which they live of student progress. It means school district curriculum departments undertaking the difficult task of creating benchmarks that describe the information and technology skills students are expected to have at various grade levels and designing the assessment tools needed to measure progress toward those benchmarks. It means finding ways to aggregate the assessed benchmark data to determine how well the entire program or school is doing. It means using technology to build personal portfolios of thoughtful, creative work that students and teachers can share with parents; to present worthwhile and authoritative reports to classmates; and to make meaningful efforts aimed at solving genuine personal, school, or community problems. It means adopting an approach to information and technology "literacy" for all students that is taken as seriously as is the teaching of reading, writing, and mathematics. It means being able to determine if the use of technology is making our children better citizens, better consumers, better communicators, better thinkers—better people.

As a teacher, use this checklist to determine how your district is meeting your student technology use needs:

❑ **1.** Integrated uses of school-adopted, stand-alone skill practice and simulation software titles to meet curricular goals

❑ **2.** Planned use of proven computerized instructional systems that have been formally adopted by curriculum departments

❑ **3.** Integrated curricular use of subject-specific technologies, such as science probes, graphing calculators, accounting software, computer-assisted design programs, and so on

❑ **4.** Planned use of adaptive technologies for students with special needs

❑ **5.** Planned use of reading promotion software

❑ **6.** Written information literacy skills curriculum that includes grade-level benchmarks (K–12) in research and technology use

❑ **7.** Units at each grade level that are team-taught by classroom teachers and library media or technology integration specialists and that are tied to the information and technology literacy curriculum

❑ **8.** Assessment tools for information literacy units

❑ **9.** Method of reporting students' attainment of information literacy and technology skills to individual students and parents

❑ **10.** Method of aggregating information literacy and technology skill attainment and reporting results to the school board and community

❑ **11.** Plan for continuous assessment and for revision of the information and technology literacy curriculum

❑ **12.** Plan for teaching and assessing safe and ethical technology use by students

❑ **13.** Opportunities for students to participate in distance learning

❑ **14.** Opportunities for students to experiment with new and emerging technologies and alternate uses of technologies as learning tools

A district that addresses each level of a technology hierarchy that is planned and shared with all school staff and the community can help answer and reduce statements like those that began this section on establishing framework for thinking about technology in schools. Such a framework can change the question from Should I use technology in teaching? to How can I use technology to improve the educational experience of my students? It can lead to better budgeting, more effective staff development planning, and an understanding by teachers and administrators of all the roles technology can play in helping make our schools more effective.

Gone Missing

There are a number of workers I rarely see anymore . . .

- I don't see parking attendants when entering or leaving a lot. My credit card talks to a machine on the way in and again on the way out.

- I don't talk to check-in people at the airline counters anymore. My credit card talks to a terminal that prints out my boarding pass. That is, if I haven't already checked in online and printed my pass at home.

- I am seeing fewer bank tellers and grocery store clerks. My debit card talks to the ATM and to the cash register at the supermarket after I have scanned my own groceries.

- My children think I am telling tall tales when I tell them I once had "people" who pumped my gas, washed my car windows, filled my tires, and sometimes gave me a free tumbler as a gift when I went to a *service* station.

- I don't hear the voice of a human telephone operator, tech support person, or reservation clerk until I've waded through a half dozen phone menus. And as often as not these voices are coming from Bangalore, India.

On the next page is a chart with the sexy title "Trends in Tasks Done by the U.S. Workforce 1969–1998 (1969 = 0)" from way back in 2004.

Parking lot attendants and their kindred who have gone missing fall into the "routine cognitive work" and "routine manual work" categories. The information that attendants and the like gave—and the processes they performed—were all standardized, multiple-choice answers, if you will. If any situation arose that called for something more than an A, B, C, or D response, a supervisor was found.

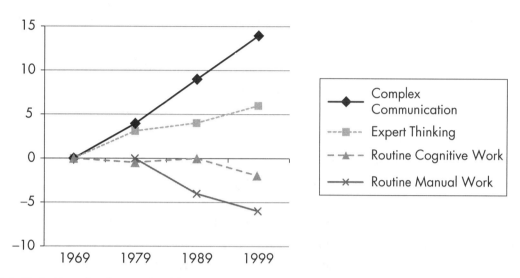

Trends in Tasks Done by the U.S. Workforce 1969–1998 (1969 = 0)
Source: **F. Levy and R. Murnane, "Education and the Changing Job Market,"** *Educational Leadership,* **October 2004,** *62*(2), **81.**

So, a couple of questions . . .

1. Are teachers vulnerable to these shifts in the labor market? Will teachers who are only information dispensers, book readers, babysitters, and multiple-choice-quiz givers be automated and "go missing"?

    Have you asked yourself lately which of the tasks you spend your time on are routine? Do most things you do require professional judgment, problem solving, and, yes, creativity? What do you provide that an online resource can't?

    If *all* educators don't attend to adding value as expert thinkers and complex communicators, if they don't rebel against "teacher-proof" classroom models, fact-heavy mandated curricula, and objective basic skills testing as a sole measure of student performance, the deprofessionalization of our jobs may well come sooner rather than later.

    It's human nature to grouse a bit when confronted by a problem at work. Perhaps we ought to be grateful instead, if problems are what allow us to demonstrate our complex communication and expert thinking skills, which in turn helps to ensure our jobs.

2. Are we giving our students experience practicing "complex communication" and "expert thinking" skills in their assignments? Daniel Pink, in his book *Drive*

(2010), suggests that all teachers ask these questions about the homework they give (p. 164):

- Am I offering students any autonomy over how and when to do this work?

- Does this assignment promote mastery by offering a novel, engaging task (as opposed to rote reformulation of something already covered in class)?

- Do my students understand the purpose of the assignment? That is, can they see how doing this additional activity at home contributes to the larger enterprise in which the class is engaged?

If we genuinely believe future workers need to be creative problem solvers, why do we still give objective tests measuring the recall of trivia and only assess low-level, basic skills on such a regular basis? Do we construct information and technology literacy projects that honestly call for higher-order thinking skills—or are we asking only for a simple regurgitation of disassociated facts? Do we ask our students to communicate complex ideas and with complex media?

I keep thinking about a prediction made in the mid-1990s by a federal Department of Education official. She suggested that one day schools for the economically disadvantaged would be full of computers (drill and practice machines, programmed learning dispensers, evaluators), whereas wealthy schools would have human teachers (mentors, guides, challengers). Ironic at the time; more accurate today than we might think.

Those being trained by automatons to be automatons will be among the first to go missing in tomorrow's job market.

CHAPTER TWO

Q&A About Some Basics

This chapter answers questions I often get from teachers about personal and classroom technologies—hardware, software, and online resources. But a warning: if you are reading this book much more than a few years after its publication date, double-check this information. Hardware, software, and Web resources are constantly changing.

What Type of Computer Should I Have?

You need a computer both at work and at school unless you really like to spend long hours tied to your classroom computer or you have managed to get a laptop computer as part of your teaching job. Even if you do have a school laptop, a home computer is essential if you have others at home (especially children) who need a computer, if you want to use a computer for personal business, or if you find that your technology department too strictly limits what you can do with a school computer.

You probably will not get a choice of computer at school, but you can choose your home machine. There are a number of factors to consider when buying a computer.

> **Survival tip:** Purchase the same kind of computer your most computer-savvy friend or relative owns. You will have built-in tech support. You might also consider purchasing a computer running the same operating system your computer at school uses so you can concentrate on learning one system well.

WHAT OPERATING SYSTEM (OS) SHOULD I CHOOSE: WINDOWS, MACINTOSH, GNU/LINUX, OR CHROME?

There are several choices of operating systems.

Microsoft Windows OS is the most popular operating system throughout the world. Most businesses run on Windows. Windows runs on many computer models, including the popular Dell, HP, Sony, and Lenovo systems as well as many budget-model computers. More software titles are written for this OS than any other, and it is rare to find computer software that will not run on Windows.

Windows has some drawbacks. It tends to be more complicated to use than some other systems, such as Apple's Macintosh OS, although with each release Windows and Macintosh grow increasingly similar. Due to its popularity, Microsoft Windows OS is targeted by more viruses, spyware, and other nasty security threats than other operating systems that are less popular, so users need to be more conscious of security measures necessary to protect their system.

Apple's Macintosh OS is often popular in schools. It runs, however, only on hardware that Apple itself manufactures, which tends to be more expensive initially. There is a lot of software written for the Mac OS, but one occasionally finds applications that are Windows-only. Check with your school's tech department to see if a Mac will run all the software you need to use.

Survival tip: There are commercial programs, such as Boot Camp or Parallels Desktop for Mac, that can be installed on the Macintosh operating system that run Windows and Windows programs.

Although Macs tend to cost more per machine, they have a long life and are often competitively priced when comparing speeds and memory specifications. They tend to be less susceptible to viruses, spyware, and other malicious pieces of computer code, although they are not 100 percent immune. Apple specializes in graphics applications, especially digital video editing and graphic design, so if you are a creative person, a Mac might be for you.

The open-source **GNU/Linux OS** is popular among people who really like to mess with computers. Its being open-source means that it is free to use and modify (see the section What Are Freeware and Open-Source Software? in this chapter), but most people use an established brand of GNU/Linux, such as Red Hat or Ubuntu, that may have a cost. Schools often use GNU/Linux on servers to run other open-source programs, such as Web servers or course management systems like Moodle. GNU/Linux runs on about any machine that will run Windows, including older computers with less memory and slower processing speeds, but check before you buy.

Google Chrome OS is the newest OS on the market. It is free and is designed to run on low-powered netbooks and tablets with most work done directly on the

Internet (cloud computing is discussed later in this chapter). This is a fast and low-cost option for basic computer use—for example, e-mailing, social networking, and using online productivity tools, such as Google Apps—but it will not support machine-based software, such as Microsoft Office, Apple's iWork, or OpenOffice.org. Most people use Chrome on their second, more portable computing device.

HOW MUCH MEMORY DO I NEED, AND HOW FAST DOES THE COMPUTER NEED TO RUN?

Computing devices have three main specifications: processor speed, random-access memory (RAM), and hard drive capacity.

Processing speed determines how fast programs open and respond to commands. RAM is the amount of memory used while the machine is operating. Get as fast a computer processor with as much RAM as you can afford because program demands continually grow.

Hard drive space determines how many programs and files you can store on the computer. Luckily, hard drives have grown very large without increasing much in cost. Unless you plan to store most of your work on the Internet itself and work online most of the time, a fairly large hard drive is an inexpensive investment. You can also purchase inexpensive external hard drives, often not much larger than a deck of cards, for storing little-used files and for making those important backup copies of your files. A recent trend has been to replace mechanical hard drives with internal flash drives that are fast, are more durable, and require less power. They tend to be smaller and more costly than mechanical hard drives and are mostly used in portable computing devices.

Serious gamers and graphic designers should also look into video RAM—memory dedicated to running high-end graphics.

DESKTOP, LAPTOP, NETBOOK, OR TABLET?

The **desktop computer**—a big, plastic box with a large monitor—is the traditional personal computing device. It has the advantage of being the most powerful, least expensive, and most customizable kind of computer that can be purchased. It usually connects to the Internet using a wired (Ethernet) connection and will run the greatest number of programs. The disadvantage, of course, is that you have to go to the computer. It doesn't come with you, not easily anyway.

Laptop computers—portable but powerful devices—are an increasingly popular tool for educators, especially those who may work in multiple classrooms or buildings. These devices can also be taken home and to conferences or meetings. They are more expensive and usually less powerful than desktop computers, but they still run most popular computer applications. They are also more susceptible to damage and loss, are more difficult to upgrade, and tend to have a shorter life span.

In late 2008 eight of the ten best-selling computers on Amazon were **netbooks.** Netbooks share these characteristics:

- Light weight—two to four pounds
- Small screen—seven to ten inches
- Static memory or a small hard drive
- Somewhat smaller than full-sized keyboard
- Wireless Internet connectivity
- Webcam, microphone, and speaker
- USB ports and memory card slot
- Price of less than $400

Netbooks come with a limited version of Windows or some flavor of the open-source operating system GNU/Linux. They often come bundled with an open-source productivity suite like OpenOffice.org and an open-source Web browser like Firefox. Be aware that netbook operating systems are often limited in functionality.

Although these devices do allow users to work offline writing papers, using spreadsheets, and designing slide show presentations, they are really designed to be used in a cloud computing environment with the bulk of the work done online.

The most recent entry in the computing device market is the **tablet,** of which Apple's iPad, Dell's Streak, and the Motorola Xoom are popular early models. Many smartphones have similar operating systems running iOS or Android operating systems. Most teachers will find tablets to be wonderful for basic communication, information retrieval, and media consumption (watching movies or listening to music), but will probably find them too limited to be their only computer. Tablet owners usually use a touch screen rather than a keyboard and mouse for interactions.

WHAT OTHER EQUIPMENT SHOULD I BUY?

Most teachers will want some additional tools to use with the computer itself.

We still have yet to achieve the oft-prophesied "paperless" society, so you will need a **printer.** There are two basic choices: inkjet and laser. Inkjet printers are inexpensive to purchase but expensive to keep filled with ink. Laser printers, especially those that print color, are expensive to purchase but less expensive to use, especially when printing a lot of copies. Calculate your "total cost of ownership" based on how much printing you plan to do.

A good **digital camera,** either still or video, is easy to use and inexpensive to purchase. You will want digital cameras for both home and school use. The video and still cameras built into cell phones are of increasingly better quality and may be sufficient to meet your classroom needs.

Survival tip: Make sure you have a signed parent release form before putting any student picture on a public Web site. Never include full names or student e-mail addresses.

A basic flatbed **scanner** converts your paper documents and photos into computer documents quickly and easily. Many scanners come with optical character recognition software that will convert a graphic full of text into an editable document. The success of converting a graphic to text will in large part depend on the quality and complexity of the original document.

Attaching an **external hard drive** to your computer allows you to make all-important backup copies of your files. You can also use this to keep your files current and synchronized if used on multiple computers.

WHAT BASIC SOFTWARE DO I NEED?

Computers are expensive paperweights without good software. Most teachers will need these tools to be professionally productive.

A **suite of productivity tools,** including a word processor and a spreadsheet and presentation program, is essential. The granddaddy and still most popular program for the majority of computer users is Microsoft Office. The academic version, usually discounted for educators and students, has a robust word processor that can do some page-layout work, a spreadsheet application with the ability to generate graphs and charts, and a presentation program with the ability to import and display multimedia (graphics, sounds, and movies). Apple's iWork programs are similar, but they only run on Macintosh computers. OpenOffice.org is an open-source, free product that is surprisingly full-featured.

A **recent Web browser** is also a necessity. The most widely used Web browser is Microsoft's Internet Explorer. It has real competition though from Mozilla Firefox, Google Chrome, and Apple's Safari. These programs are free, so try them all. The Web browsers that are the most functional use plug-ins, small programs that work within the browser to do specialized tasks like adding functionality to online e-mail programs, opening different types of files, providing online security, and blocking annoying pop-up messages in Web pages.

Photo editing and organizing software is a useful addition. Adobe Photoshop has been the application of choice for those who are truly into working with digital photographs. It has a less powerful and less expensive version, Adobe Photoshop

Elements. Another program, iPhoto, comes standard on Macintosh computers and offers the basic photo editing capabilities of cropping, resizing, adjusting colors, and eliminating red-eye in addition to helping teachers organize and share photographs. There are many free online and open-source photo editing and organizing tools available as well.

An **electronic grade book** is essential for teachers. Most districts will require the use of a specific grade book that is often tied to the school's student information system. A place for recording end-of-term grades, an attendance function, and a parent-student portal into the grade book are often parts of the best grade books. These are becoming Web based, meaning that you can work on them from any computer, not just the one on your desk.

An **e-mail client,** such as Microsoft Outlook (a part of Microsoft Office) or Apple's Mail and iMail, helps teachers send, read, store, and organize e-mail. Gmail, a part of Google Apps for Education, does similar tasks but is accessed through a Web browser. These programs usually include a **calendar, address book,** and **to-do list.**

A **PDF reader** opens the ubiquitous Adobe PDF (Portable Document Format) files. The free Adobe Reader performs this function, as does Apple's Preview software.

Survival tip: You can copy and paste text from a PDF into other documents, where it can be modified. Mac OS lets you create PDF files of any document using the "print" and then "save as" PDF operations.

What Are Freeware and Open-Source Software?

Most teachers are always looking for ways to save money. Here's one means of economizing—stop buying computer software.

No, I am not advocating becoming a pirate. Johnny Depp can pull it off, but I don't recommend it for educators. (Too few of us look that good in mascara.) Instead, take a serious look at some high-quality software that is now available—at *no* cost.

And just how can they do it for such a low, low price? you might be asking. There are basically three types of "free" software:

- **Open-source software** uses code that the creator has placed in the public domain and that users then rewrite and improve. The GNU/Linux operating system is probably the most famous open-source product available.

- **Versions of commercial products with minimal features** are made available by a producer who then hopes that features available only in the purchased version will sell the software. The Web-based application Animoto operates this way.

- **Web-based software applications** that derive revenue from advertising are growing in popularity. Yahoo! Mail uses this economic model.

The following list of sample free computer programs is useful and reliable for the average computer user. All run on multiple computer platforms and have good track records of reliability:

1. Audacity allows the user to edit sound files.
2. GIMPshop is photo editing software similar to Adobe Photoshop.
3. Inkscape is a drawing program comparable to Adobe Illustrator.
4. OpenOffice.org has many of the same tools as Microsoft Office, and it is compatible with Word, Excel, and PowerPoint.
5. Scribus is desktop publishing software similar to Microsoft Publisher.
6. Tux Paint works much like the children's drawing program Kid Pix.

Survival tip: Before acquiring any software, check with your technology department or media specialist. Consideration of compatibility and support issues as well as program licenses currently in place will save you time, money, and frustration.

Here are a few of the dozens of online tools you might find useful:

1. Google Reader organizes all your blogs and RSS feeds.
2. Delicious organizes your bookmarks.
3. Flickr is an online photo album and photo-sharing application.
4. Google Docs allows you to do word processing and create spreadsheets online. Many schools have adopted Google Apps for Education, which includes Google Docs and other free tools, such as e-mail and shared calendars.
5. PBworks and Wikispaces let you share your writing and allow others to edit it as well.
6. Ta-da List lets you get organized with an online to-do list.

Of course, free and no-cost software programs have drawbacks as well. You will need to ask yourself if free software really does have both the features and the reliability you need to get your tasks accomplished. Sometimes you do get what you pay for. Also, as educators, you might be concerned by a commercial presence, such as a bit of advertising with your e-mail.

But if you (or your district) are strapped for software funds, freeware can be a reasonable alternative to having nothing or being illegal. Give it a shot. It's not like you'll be risking a lot of money.

Survival tip: Search the Internet for Web sites that list the "best free or open-source software" for lists of free programs. Richard Byrnes's Free Technology for Teachers blog is a terrific resource for discovering the latest online programs to use with students. You'll be surprised by all that is available and how well it works.

How Do I Manage Files on Multiple Computers?

For an increasing number of teachers, having multiple computers is a bigger problem than not having any access at all. How do you make sure you are always working with the latest version of your documents?

You can move documents using a writable CD, a flash drive, or a portable hard drive. You can even make a portable hard drive your primary storage device and use it on multiple computers. But remember, a physical storage device can be forgotten or lost, and you still need to keep two copies of your important work on two separate devices, preferably in two separate locations.

Teachers are increasingly finding that they can take advantage of online storage to keep organized. They can do this with Google Docs, for example: the latest version of the file is always online, where it can be either modified directly or downloaded, modified, and uploaded.

Apple's iCloud allows people who use multiple Apple products—iPads, iPods, and Apple desktop and laptop computers—to quickly synchronize music, photos, and other files among devices.

Other programs, such as Dropbox (a limited version is free), install a small program on each computer that creates a folder into which you place your documents. Dropbox uploads the most recent version of these documents to an online storage space each time you connect to the Internet—automatically. I love it!

What Is Cloud Computing, and What Are Its Advantages and Disadvantages?

- I am writing entire chapters of this book without the aid of a word processor.
- I am using several computers in several locations to write them without using a flash drive to move the files.

- I will share these chapters with editors without sending them as e-mail attachments.
- I will save my electronic chapter drafts in a place where even if my laptop is lost, the external hard drive where I keep my backups fails, and the next version of Office decides not to open earlier file formats, I will still have access to the content.
- I am able to do all of these things at no cost.

Anyone who has used Google Docs, a set of online productivity tools that allows the creation of documents, spreadsheets, presentations, and surveys, has experienced cloud computing. Cloud computing is a trend to watch because it has the potential of offering staff and students better services at a lower cost than current technology deployment models. Cloud computing relies on applications and file storage that reside on a network—either a local area network, a district intranet, or the Internet itself—with minimal resources stored on the local computer's hard drive. (A cloud graphic is often used to represent the Internet on network diagrams, hence the name.) If you have ever stored a file online, edited a photo with an online tool, or used a Web-based e-mail program, you have already experienced cloud computing.

There are several real advantages to cloud computing. Because both applications and personal documents reside on a network rather than on a specific computer, you can work on any project, anywhere, regardless of the computer being used. Given a computer with Internet access—whether it is on one's desk at school, on one's lap at home, in any computer lab or coffee shop in the world, or at Grandpa's house—one can work without worrying about transporting files on flash drives, keeping track of the latest version of a document, or having the right software to open a file. Files are easily shared and collaboratively edited in a cloud-based application as well.

Unlike most software programs that reside on computer hard drives, Web-based applications that perform a wide array of productivity tasks are provided at no cost to the user. Although not as comprehensive as Microsoft Office or Adobe Photoshop, these tools often have a surprisingly full set of features and are compatible with commercial programs.

Cloud computing can be done on computers, such as netbooks, that are less powerful than others. A school district's computing costs can be lowered using only these computers to access the cloud. Netbooks are inexpensive, file storage is free, and basic applications are free. Money that would have been spent on student workstations in labs, big file servers, and expensive software can now be used to pay for increased bandwidth, greater wireless coverage, or maybe, just maybe, lower class sizes.

One-to-one student-to-computer plans are more feasible using cloud computing. When a school uses low-cost netbooks and the cloud, student computers are virtually interchangeable—so if a device needs repair or is left at home, another machine can be easily substituted. The only application needed on a netbook is a full-fledged Web browser. I predict that at some point K–12 schools will ask parents to provide basic computing devices for their children as a part of the school supply list. As a parent, I was asked to purchase a $100 graphing calculator for my son when he was in high school not long ago. How big a stretch is it to ask parents to provide a $250 netbook computer today?

HOW CAN TEACHERS TAKE ADVANTAGE OF CLOUD COMPUTING?

Before advocating for cloud computing for my district's staff and students, I decided to see if I could "live in the cloud" as a computer user myself for a few months. My personal move wasn't that difficult, even for a geezer like me. These are my top computer uses and how I have moved my tasks to the cloud:

1. **Working on a netbook.** Rather than using a full-scale laptop computer, I used a ten-inch netbook that cost about $350. The smaller keyboard and screen size took getting accustomed to, but I could work on the computer for long periods of time. The speed was acceptable, the battery life was good, and the wireless connectivity was fast.

2. **E-mailing.** Both my school and personal e-mail accounts are hosted by Gmail; I was already using this online e-mail program.

3. **Web bookmarking.** I already had a Delicious account, so I just imported the bookmarks I'd saved in my browser.

4. **Word processing, creating presentations, and using spreadsheets.** After years of using Office, the move to Google Docs for my day-to-day productivity was surprisingly easy. In fact, getting away from Office's feature creep (the continuous addition of rarely used features that leads to busy and confusing menus) has been refreshing. For 95 percent of my work and for storing my files, Google Docs works just fine, thank you. The work I create is compatible with Office as well.

5. **Editing and storing photos.** I've been storing my best photographs on a commercial storage site for years and editing them with Photoshop Elements. But Flickr and Picasa Web are online applications that work just fine for my amateur editing and storage needs. Picasa Web gives iPhoto a run for its money as a photo organizer. And Picnik affords me even more photo editing abilities.

6. **Web page editing and webmastering.** My personal blog, wiki, and Web site are already completely managed via application service providers that use online tools for management and editing. As is our school Web site. As are the professional association Web sites I help manage—those of my local Kiwanis club, our lakes association, and our state library and tech association.

7. **Completing school-specific tasks.** All grade books, reporting systems, and forms of communication in our district are Web based, as are our student management, individual education plan, and library systems. Most course management tools, such as Moodle, are Web based.

As cloud computing gained maturity and acceptance, our district looked for an appropriate "enterprise" solution that would provide a common set of tools and storage to all staff and students. We gave all staff and students access to Google Apps for Education in 2010 at no cost to the district. So far, so good. Microsoft offers a similar set of online tools as well in its Office 365 for education product.

DISADVANTAGES OF CLOUD COMPUTING

So what is the downside of this approach to providing computer resources to oneself and one's staff and students? Why shouldn't everyone fly to the cloud right now? There are some questions that need serious consideration:

- **What happens when there is no Internet access?** Google Docs and Gmail can be used offline using the Chrome browser. You can work without an Internet connection and your documents will be synced when the next Internet connection is made. Bandwidth limitations may be a challenge for some districts.

- **Am I abetting Google's world domination? Might there someday be a charge for these now "free" services?** Definitely "yes" on the world domination question. Just accept it and get over it. If you feel uncomfortable using Google or Microsoft, there are alternatives like Zoho. The sustainability of the revenue model is anybody's guess. Profits now come from advertisements and selling more full-featured versions of applications or larger storage spaces.

- **Are my files secure?** This is probably the deal-breaker for many skeptics of this trend. As a devout belt-and-suspenders kind of guy, I'd encourage you to keep local backup copies of all important online documents. But so far there have been only minor reported instances of security problems, data loss, or interruptions in these services.

- **Are my files private?** Can we trust Google and others not to peek at our stuff? This is another major concern. On its "Security & Privacy" page, Google Apps for Education clearly spells out its privacy policy. Read it. I am personally convinced that my data are secure, private, and my own. I would certainly study the privacy settings of any online program I might use—who gets access to what is getting more customizable all the time. My own insurance against problems associated with unwarranted data access is living a completely sin-free life. But I know that won't work for everyone.

- **Are there some things just too cumbersome to do online?** I recognize that if I were editing videos I'd need a full-blown computer. I can't play or make CDs or DVDs. Any big data crunching tasks still need lots of computing power. Cloud computing is not for every computing need.

It's a good time to consider the impact of cloud computing and netbooks on our classrooms, libraries, and school systems. With such a low (and dropping) cost, I'd bet dollars to doughnuts that even in these tough economic times quite a number of students will be getting their hands on netbooks.

Remember that every cloud does have a silver lining!

What Does a Technologically Well-Equipped Classroom Look Like?

A pundit once speculated that should a nineteenth-century physician be transported to the present day, she or he would not recognize a modern operating room. A nineteenth-century banker would not be able to function in today's bank. In fact, the writer observed, the only professional whose working environment would have changed so little that she or he could begin working immediately would be the public classroom teacher. The practices and technology of teaching have changed that little in the past couple hundred years.

How long this remains even somewhat true is quickly changing in many districts. Whereas changes in teaching practices are less observable, changes in classroom technologies are dramatic in those schools with vision, commitment, and, well, funding. My first classroom in the mid-1970s had a chalkboard, and I could check out an overhead projector, filmstrip projector, or 16 mm projector from the library. Compare this to today's "smart" classrooms that contain the following:

- **Telephones.** A POT (Plain Old Telephone) with a voice mailbox remains the essential "information appliance." It's amazing to me how many classrooms still do not have this "luxury."

Survival tip: If you don't have a telephone, use Skype or Gmail to place telephone calls using your networked computer. Computer-to-computer calls are free; calls from computers to land lines or cell phones cost very little. Videoconferencing is also easily done using these products. They're great for giving your students who may be out of school for extended periods of time opportunities to reconnect with you and their classmates.

- **Networked teacher computers.** Whether for keeping grades, creating study materials, creating multimedia presentations, or communicating with e-mail, a computer for each teacher is an essential teaching tool. An increasing number of teachers are gaining access to laptop or tablet computers that can be used from multiple locations in the classroom as well as outside it.

- **Data projectors.** The ability to project the image of a computer screen so the entire class can view it is essential. As lessons become Web based, educational films are streamed (delivered digitally), and teacher-created multimedia presentations reach today's visual learners, the computer becomes a tool for whole-group instruction with the availability of a data projector—preferably mounted permanently in the classroom.

- **Interactive whiteboards.** These devices, which work in conjunction with a computer and data projector, allow the user to write in "digital" ink, record the writings as a computer file, and use the surface of the interactive whiteboard as a touch screen. They come with highly interactive programs that allow students to manipulate projected images. Once you've used one, you will never want to do without it.

- **Student response systems.** Sold in sets of twenty or thirty, these small handheld devices allow students to send specific information to a program that then records and reports the responses of each student during a lesson. These can greatly enhance the interactivity of the class, thereby increasing engagement. Asking multiple-choice questions and conducting opinion polls to check for understanding are popular uses of these devices. Some colleges are requiring students to purchase their own response device. (You might also hear these referred to as "clickers.")

Survival tip: There are Web-based programs, such as Poll Everywhere, that allow students to use their own cell phones as response devices using text messaging—a no-cost solution for schools that can't afford the commercial hardware. Note that there may be a text messaging charge for the owner of the cell phone.

- **Sound amplification systems.** Classrooms with students with hearing loss or large classrooms benefit from the amplification of the teacher's voice using a wireless microphone and sound system.

- **Document cameras.** These simple devices that connect to data projectors or TV monitors allow teachers to show either print documents or objects using a camera. Some can be attached to microscopes for viewing by the class.

- **Student mini-labs or portable wireless labs.** If schools are to give students ready access to computing for research, for communication, or for engaging with educational computer games and simulations, student computers will need to be in the classroom—either permanently in mini-labs or temporarily through wireless labs. Smaller devices, such as tablets and netbooks, are growing in popularity for this type of use.

In the not-too-distant future, teachers will view these (and other) instructional technologies as being critical to their job, just as yesterday's teachers viewed the chalkboard. Digital technologies will be required to reach and teach our "digital native" learners.

Seven Stupid Mistakes Teachers Make with Technology

Stupid is as stupid does.

—*Forrest Gump*

Stupid is not my favorite word. It sounds mean, harsh, and ugly. But after reading in *Newsweek* that 25 percent of employees visit porn sites from work and that the adult video industry claims hits on porn sites are highest during the workday, it was truly the only term that seemed to fit this sort of human behavior.

I use the term *stupid* under fairly constrained conditions. To me, a stupid act has a degree of willfulness about it and is serious. Making an error once is ignorance; making the same mistake multiple times is stupidity. Unfortunately, I see stupid acts and beliefs related to technology in schools way too often.

These would be my nominees for the most stupid things a teacher can do related to technology:

1. **Not backing up data.** "You mean having two copies of my files on the hard drive doesn't count as a backup?" The first time a teacher loses his or her precious data, my heart breaks. The second time, well, stupidity ought to cause some suffering.

Survival tip: Many operating systems come with an automated backup system to be used with an external hard drive. Ask your technician to help set up such a system for you. That $100 you spend on the extra drive will seem cheap if (or should I say when) your computer crashes.

2. **Treating a school computer like a home computer.** Teachers who use a school computer to run a business, edit their kid's wedding videos, or send tasteless jokes to half of North America (including that fundamentalist math teacher down the hall) are being stupid. Teachers who take their computers home and let their kids hack on them are being stupid. Teachers who don't own a personal computer for personal business deserve to get into trouble.

3. **Not supervising computer-using students.** It is really stupid to believe Internet filters will keep kids out of trouble on the Internet. Even the kids who can't get around the school's filter can still exploit that 10 percent of porn sites the filter won't catch if they choose to do so. They can still send cyberbullying e-mail messages—maybe even using your e-mail address. Or they can just plain waste time.

4. **Thinking online communication is ever private.** Eventually everyone sends an embarrassing personal message to an electronic mailing list. I've heard of some tech directors who get their jollies reading salacious interstaff e-mail. Your school e-mail messages can be requested and must be produced if germane to any federal lawsuits. Even e-mail deleted from your computer still sits on servers somewhere—often for a very loooong time. Think you wiped out your browsing history? Don't bet that that is the only set of tracks you've left that show where you've been surfing. Your Facebook page will be looked at by the school board chair; your superintendent and principal know who the author of that "anonymous" blog is. Not assuming others can see what you send and do online is stupid.

5. **Believing that one's teaching style need not change to take full advantage of technology.** Using technology to simply add sounds and pictures to lectures is stupid. Smart technology use is about changing the roles of both teacher and student. The computer-using student can now be the content expert; the teacher becomes the process expert, asking such questions as "Where did you get that information?" "How do you know it's accurate?" "Why is it important?" "How can you let others know what you discovered?" and "How can you tell if you did a good job?" The world has changed, and it is stupid not to recognize it and change as well.

6. **Ignoring the intrinsic interest in tech use among today's kids.** Kids like technology. Not using it as a hook to motivate and interest them in their education is stupid.

7. **Thinking technology in schools will go away.** The expectation that "this too shall pass" has worked for a lot of educational practices and theories. Madeline Hunter, outcomes-based education, whole-language reading instruction, and (soon) NCLB all had their day in the sun before being pushed aside. But it is stupid to think technology will go away in education. It isn't going away in banking, medicine, business, science, and agriculture—anywhere else in society. Anticipating that "this too shall pass" about technology is pretty stupid.

Seven Brilliant Things Teachers Do with Technology

Our deepest fear is not that we are inadequate. Our deepest fear is that we are powerful beyond measure. It is our light, not our darkness, that most frightens us.

—*Marianne Williamson, 1996, p. 190*

I just listed seven stupid mistakes teachers make with technology. Easy marks, you teachers.

But, to be fair, I see just as many or even more brilliant teacher uses of technology. Here are some practices that just make me marvel and feel proud to be a part of the profession:

1. **Empowering kids with technology.** Technology is an amplifier of natural abilities. By helping their students harness technology, brilliant teachers see that good writers become better writers, good debaters become better debaters, good French speakers become better French speakers, good mathematical problem solvers become better mathematical problem solvers, and so on. They see technology not as a crutch but as a propellant. Brilliant teachers have themselves experienced the empowering effect of technology. Brilliant teachers use good assessment strategies to rigorously determine the quality of technology-enhanced projects.

2. **Creatively finding and using resources.** I can't believe the technologies found in some of our district's classrooms that were neither provided by our department nor stolen (I don't think). Through personal purchase, through parent-teacher groups, through grants, through business partnerships, through parental contacts, through fundraising, and through classroom supply budgets, brilliant teachers amazingly amass digital cameras and clickers and sensors and classroom computer labs. One of our brilliant teachers MacGyver-ed his own document camera out of an old camcorder, plastic pipe, and duct tape.

3. **Making conferencing real-time.** Brilliant teachers don't wait until scheduled parent conferences to communicate with homes. Through e-mail, Web sites, online grade books, blogs, wikis, and, yes, even telephone calls, technology gives teachers the ability to help make parents partners who assist them in ensuring students' timely completion of quality work. These teachers post newsletters, spelling lists, assessment tools, assignments, grades, calendars, discussion lists, and tips. They read and respond to parent e-mail messages. Most parents *want* to be involved, but they need to know *how*.

4. **Putting kids in touch with the world.** The classrooms of brilliant teachers (hokey metaphor alert) have no walls. These teachers "get" the "flat world" challenge, understanding that tomorrow's citizens and workers will have an advantage if they can work successfully with other cultures. From "keypals" from back in the day to Vicki Davis's Flat Classroom® Project today, brilliant teachers give even the most remote students a glimpse and a dream of the bigger world—and help them both communicate and empathize with those in it.

5. **Accepting the role of colearner.** One of the best signs of intelligent people is that they tend to willingly admit when they don't know something. Brilliant teachers not only accept the dismal fact that they will never know all there is to know about technology but also turn the condition into a classroom advantage by having their brilliant children teach them how to do something techie now and then.

> **Survival tip:** Always consider yourself a colearner with your students on any project that involves technology. Students learn by teaching, not just by being taught.

6. **Using the kids' own devices to teach them.** Brilliant teachers understand this old Arab proverb: "It's easier to steer the camel in the direction it is already heading." Students are increasingly and unstoppably bringing in personal communication devices—cell phones, cameras, game devices, iPods and MP3 players, netbooks, laptops, and PDAs. Brilliant teachers know how to use cell phones to poll their classes; create podcasts of lectures for later review; use games to teach difficult concepts; and make "Google jockeys" of student wireless laptop users.

7. **Delighting in the discovery, the newness, and the fun technology holds.** It's not about technology. It's about finding out about and doing "cool" things. We knew that ourselves as kids. Brilliant tech-using teachers have never lost the thrill of doing something new and interesting with these

electronic Tinkertoys. They are pleased with their tech-using students and pleased with themselves. Brilliant teachers use technology's engagement (not entertainment) power. Technology is not "just one more thing" but a vital experience that brings discovery, excitement, and even fun to the classroom.

Technology won't make a poor teacher a good one. But it can make a good teacher even better. And it can help make great teachers whose students remember them for the rest of their lives.

What brilliant uses will *you* make of technology?

CHAPTER THREE

Using Technology for Professional Productivity

Chapters Three, Four, and Five of this book will describe a natural progression of technology use by teachers:

- Using technology for professional productivity
- Using technology to enhance traditional teaching practices
- Using technology to teach 21st-century skills

These uses are cumulative. Although most teachers progress through these stages, they continue to practice all uses.

As I indicated in the introduction to this book, my own realization that technology could empower my students was the direct result of being empowered by a single technology: the word processor. For most of us, until we see how a computer application, a Web site, or a device makes us more productive; makes an activity more engaging; or makes a task easier to accomplish, it is impossible to share that technology with students.

Survival tip: Use only the technologies that personally empower you with your students. You can't teach a language you don't know; you shouldn't share a book you don't like; and you can't teach in a way in which you are not a successful learner. It's the same with technology.

Keeping Professionally Organized: Managing the Business of Teaching

It seems a contradiction. Although the amount of information we deal with on the job grows daily, the number of secretaries, who once answered phones, sent letters, typed reports, kept our schedules, and filed and retrieved information, has shrunk. Who is doing the work of the missing secretaries?

Efficient teachers directly handle communication through voice and e-mail; compose, file, and retrieve letters and reports using word processors; track budgets through spreadsheets and online accounting systems; and access school-specific data using student information systems and grade books. We are our own secretaries—thanks to technology.

Teachers have, of course, always had responsibility for their own calendars, address books, and to-do lists. Such electronic organizers as Microsoft Outlook and Google Apps for Education's Gmail have four functions that work with their primary function as e-mail programs:

1. **Calendar.** An electronic calendar can be used to schedule single appointments and daylong events as well as repeating appointments, and it gives a visual or auditory alert prior to scheduled meetings. A shared calendaring system makes scheduling meetings easier because an open block of time for all attendees can be located quickly. Multiple calendars are easy to create that can be color-coded—one for school events, one for your extracurricular activities, one for personal events, and so on.

> **Survival tip:** I copy and paste meeting agendas directly into the notes section of the calendar event. It saves me trying to find them when the meeting is held.

Shared calendars can also be used to schedule the use of shared facilities, such as computer labs, conference rooms, or other workspaces in the school.

2. **Address book.** Like its paper cousin, the electronic address book keeps names, addresses, phone numbers, birthdays, e-mail addresses, and other helpful information, but it is easily updated and can be used in conjunction with an e-mail program to automate the addressing of messages and adding new contacts.

3. **To-do list.** The electronic to-do list can help users prioritize tasks; store completed tasks for later reference; and track additional information, such as due dates.

4. **Means of making this information available and portable.** Electronic organizers contain information that is needed when one is away from the computer. Good organizers ...

- Format and print selected data on sheets that fit in paper organizers.

- Synchronize with smartphones and other handheld computing devices. Student information system data can also be downloaded into such devices, allowing a student's schedule to be checked outside the office.

- Store the organized data on a Web server that can be accessed through the Internet. (See the discussion of cloud computing in Chapter Two.)

Communicating Using Technology

Teachers can use technology to become more effective communicators, improving the flow of information to and from other staff members, students, parents, and the community.

- Modern telephone systems that extend into the classroom are vital for two-way communication with students' homes. Voice mail greetings with informative introductions ("Today is February 12th. I will be in class all day, but can take calls after 3:00 PM") help end frustrating rounds of telephone tag. The best telephone systems automatically route calls to voice mail during instructional times and allow those outside the building to call specific extensions without going through a receptionist. Some systems now route calls to another extension or even a cell phone when necessary.

- E-mail has become the communication method of choice for many teachers and parents. Quick, thoughtful e-mail responses to questions or concerns can take less time than telephone conversations. Sending e-mail using electronic mailing lists is an efficient way to disburse information to groups of people. This can be done either by setting up a "group" nickname in one's e-mail program for smaller e-mailings or by using an electronic mailing list for e-mailing larger, more permanent groups. Our district has separate electronic mailing lists specifically created for all staff, all administrators, all teachers, all staff in individual buildings, all district parents, and all parents of students in individual buildings.

> **Survival tip:** Check to see if your student information system has a feature that allows you to send e-mail (or text) messages to all your students' parents using the most current enrollment data. Not having to create and maintain your own mailing lists is an additional time-saver.

- Face-to-face communication can be enhanced with technology. Electronic slide shows, such as those created with PowerPoint, help both inform and persuade. Judiciously chosen text allows the listener to follow and recognize key points of the presentation. Charts, graphs, and diagrams illustrate concepts that are difficult to comprehend with words alone. Digital photographs of students and staff can convince audiences by showing how programs affect individuals and can appeal to the emotions of viewers.

  Well-directed and well-edited video is becoming increasingly easier to create because digital video cameras and computerized editing programs no longer require a high degree of expertise. An increasing number of teachers are recording their lessons and uploading them to a server on the Internet so students can watch them outside of class for review. Science teachers can bring the field into the classroom with video; history teachers can tape and show local history sites; and math teachers can record short interviews with professionals telling how they use math in their work.

- Programs on district and community cable television networks can be a great public relations tool. Informative programs and bulletin boards of activities keep the entire community aware of good things happening in schools. Video streaming—broadcasting video over the Internet—is becoming more common. Anyone can view the programming by simply going to a Web page.

- A school Web site with information that can be kept current and usable is expected by most communities. Basic contact information, calendars of events, staff directories, hot lunch menus, school policy documents, curriculum guides, and links to departments and buildings in the district are useful to parents. Student work can be shared with the public using a school Web site. Schools need good Web page guidelines, and administrators need to be familiar with them.

- Social networking tools are being used by a growing number of school districts to help keep stakeholders informed. (See the following "Are You Speaking Where Your Audience Is Listening?" sidebar.)

Are You Speaking Where Your Audience Is Listening?

Oh, for the simple days of what seemed like a single means of communication—the printed newsletter. Those of us who were "tech savvy" created our newsletters in a word processor or desktop publishing program, adding headlines and clip art.

Soon the more progressive teachers recognized that e-mail was even more effective in sending newsletters, and that's what most of us have done for the last fifteen years or so. But studies are showing that e-mail use is in decline. Perhaps we need to rethink our communication strategies—especially with our students and younger parents. We need to actually go where students and parents are reading, listening, and viewing.

Here are some new avenues for information dissemination. One convenient thing is that once a message is created it can be spread in many ways.

- A **Facebook fan page** is easy to create if you have a personal Facebook page. Because "fans" have limited access to the rest of your Facebook account, this is a safe and pretty effective way to reach those who seem to use *only* social networking for communication.

- A **blog with an RSS feed** may be more effective than a regular Web site. The interactivity of a blog will be appealing to those who like to respond to ideas.

- **Twitter** is popular among a certain segment of Internet users. The 140 characters allowed for each "tweet" are about enough to alert readers of an event or to provide a link to more substantial information posted somewhere else. Maybe 140 characters is just enough to inform your staff and students about the latest books and resources available in your classroom.

- **Text, e-mail, and voice message mass sendings (or blasts)** to large groups of people, such as all parents, all school staff, or the community, may be possible in your district. School public relations departments are the masters of sending these things out, so if you have some exciting news for parents, this may be the most effective means of sharing information. Check with your PR department or student information system manager.

- Google Apps for Education has a wonderful tool called **Google Groups** that makes sending and archiving e-mail messages to larger groups really simple. Any messages sent by members of these groups are archived for easy retrieval.

- Although I am all about the written word, clever teachers tell their stories in **ways that reach visual and auditory learners.** Do you post videos on YouTube or TeacherTube? Do you make podcasts? As long as people are walking around with things stuck in their ears, they may as well be listening to something cool about your classroom.

I am not convinced that e-mail is as dead as some might suggest. Nor am I convinced of the longevity of some of these other communication media. But I do know this: *Teachers have to have a strategy for regular and formal communication with students, other teachers, principals, and parents.*

Student Information System

Teachers are expected to use the giant database known as the student information system (SIS). Most SISs are managed by specified individuals in a district, and different staff members (principals, secretaries, members of building improvement teams, and so on) use them in different ways. As a classroom teacher, you will use the student information system to

- Report attendance and lunch counts
- Record scores and accomplishment of assignments using the system's integrated grade book
- Report end-of-term grades
- Send progress updates to parents and students
- Find demographics (parent names, addresses, phone numbers) of students
- Find student class schedules
- Find assessment data on individual students (although many districts use a more sophisticated data management or data-mining system to do this)

Survival tip: The best way to master the sometimes frustrating student information system is to find another teacher who is a "power user" in your building. He or she will often provide better information and advice than a support person who does not use the program often or in ways that a teacher does.

The most recent student information systems also give students and their parents the ability to access information on individual students through a Web "portal." This way students and parents can check on progress—assignments turned in, quiz and test scores, and project grades—in real time rather than waiting for parent-teacher conferences and report cards or having to contact you individually. Teachers can also make available upcoming assignments with dates they are due.

These portals can be a real time-saver for you, provided you keep the information in the system current, are timely in recording grades, and are conscientious about adding new assignments. Good communication with students and parents about how scores and grades are given is important.

Survival tip: Many SISs allow teachers to "roll over" assignments from one year to the next so only updating, rather than reentering a lot of information, is needed. Be careful to check the capabilities of your SIS to be sure, as information rolls over, that it updates such key information as the current semester, assignment dates, and other information that if not updated might create confusion.

Curriculum Management System

A related large system used by schools helps teachers manage the school's curriculum. At their most basic level, curriculum management systems are digital curriculum guides that describe course content and outcomes. At their more sophisticated level, they allow teachers to record and analyze individual student progress, to align the district curriculum to state and national standards, and to easily sequence skills into a continuum through grades and courses. Some student information systems now contain components of a curriculum management system to help map curricula to standards, courses, and lessons.

Course Management System

Blackboard, Desire2Learn, and open-source Moodle are examples of online tools that can help you either design classes that are taught completely online or design, organize, and make available resources and activities that supplement face-to-face classes, creating what are commonly known as "hybrid" or "blended" classes.

Although course management systems can have a steep learning curve, they can provide powerful tools, such as discussion boards, online tests and quizzes, and repositories of supplementary readings and media; they afford opportunities for collaborative learning; and they promote good student-to-student and student-to-teacher communication. In addition, they allow students to continue learning outside of class by providing twenty-four-hour access to course content and tools, such as discussion boards for student interaction and engagement.

Survival tip: So many colleges now offer classes online that states are beginning to require that all high school graduates have some experience with online learning. Becoming a Moodle guru will increase your value to your school.

School Web Site and Teacher-Created Class Pages

School districts and individual buildings use their Web sites to share a great deal of information with parents and the community. But many school Web sites also allow teachers to create individual Web pages for their classes, often using simple "fill in the blank and hit submit" forms. As a teacher, you can use these tables as a list of things to consider sharing with your Web pages.

 Survival tip: Note that some of the information in the following tables may be shared via the student information system, curriculum management system, or a general school Web site. There is no need to duplicate the information.

General Class Information	Schedule for Updating	Possibilities
Teacher's name and contact information	Annual	Your name, school phone number and extension, and e-mail address should be easy to find. Add your home phone if desired, along with the best times to contact. A personal note of welcome that includes encouragement for parents to contact the teacher if there is a question or concern is thoughtful.
Class rules and expectations	Annual	Policies on classroom behavior, homework, and extra-credit assignments should be made public. Carefully articulated and agreed upon by parents and students as reasonable, this information can reduce misunderstandings during the year.
Link to the school calendar	Annually checked	A building-created calendar based on the district calendar should show the beginning and end dates of school; holidays and breaks; days in which students are not in school for other reasons; testing schedules; and events (athletic events, open houses, field trips, science fairs, and so on).

General Class Information	Schedule for Updating	Possibilities
Supply list	Annual	This list should include paper, pencils, calculators, and other items students are expected to bring to class. Provide links to any school policy on how students without financial means can obtain school supplies and to any district school supply list.
Field trip information	As necessary	Posting online field trip descriptions, printable permission forms, costs, and calls for chaperones when necessary can simplify getting these items to parents.
Class news with photos and descriptions of current class activities	Monthly or weekly	Parents like knowing what's going on in their children's classes. List current projects, interests of students, and any special events.
Requests and guidelines for parent volunteering	Annual	Although the district, building, or parent-teacher organization may generate these, teachers who have special volunteer needs may want to let parents know.
Drop folders for student work	Annual	If students have access to the class page, a write-only drop folder for turning in work electronically has a logical place there.

Survival tip: Be careful with your class Web page—if not regularly updated, it will look old and tired. Make sure parental permissions are on file if student photos are used. No last names of students should be published.

General Class Information	Schedule for Updating	Possibilities
Class electronic mailing list	Annual, with updates as necessary	This is an easy way for a teacher to communicate quickly with all parents who have an e-mail address and, if desired, for parents to communicate with each other. Check to see if your student information system has this function—you may not need to create your own.
Counter that records the number of visits to the page	Reset annually	This counter is of value to both teachers and parents if they wish to see if the site is being used and useful.

Curriculum Information	Schedule for Updating	Possibilities
List of units taught in each subject area (elementary) or in each class (secondary)	As dictated by curricular changes	Provide a general outline of the major areas the students in the class will be studying.
State requirements met by the class or units	Updated annually or as needed	If your course covers a part of a state-mandated curriculum, this reference should be made. Include an indication of any testing the state requires to show mastery.
Projected beginning and ending dates of units	Annual	Advise parents that these dates are approximate. "We will be starting our unit on rocks and minerals just after spring break." Include tips for parents on helping keep students on track for projects.

Curriculum Information	Schedule for Updating	Possibilities
Major goals and essential learner outcomes for each unit	As dictated by curricular changes	Provide simple declarative statements of what the student should know and be able to do—sometimes referred to as essential learner outcomes. "By the end of this unit, I expect your child to be able to identify the major landmasses on Earth and be able to locate the major countries in Europe, Asia, and Africa."
Samples of final projects from previous years	Annual	These samples help give parents examples of exemplary projects as a quality indicator for their own child's work.

Unit Information	Schedule for Updating	Possibilities
Learner outcomes for units	Annual, with adjustments as needed	A detailed list of skills and information that students need to have mastered should be available.
Major activities	Annual, with adjustments as needed	List projects, readings, tests, experiments, and papers. Link these to any assessments used with the activities when possible.
Homework assignments and due dates	Weekly	Make a disclaimer for parents that due dates are subject to change. (They might be later, but never earlier.) This could serve in lieu of a lesson plan book.
Vocabulary words, spelling lists, number facts, formulas, and so on	Annual, with adjustments as needed	Include lists that call for memorization, with which parents can help students practice.
Assessments and evaluations for units and projects	Annual, with adjustments as needed	Checklists and rubrics for major projects can be useful to parents to help students self-assess their work.

Unit Information	Schedule for Updating	Possibilities
Online practice tests	Annual, with adjustments as needed	Link to any practice tests that come with standardized tests or teacher-generated tests. These tests can be created so they can be taken online or printed out.
Active links to online resources and Web pages	Annual	Online lecture notes and video recordings that you as a teacher create help both students and parents. Be sure to include links to readings, educational games, and other teacher-selected online resources.
Suggested enrichment activities with which parents can help students	Annual	Provide supplemental reading lists, enrichment activities for students who are highly motivated, or "fun" family activities that tie into the content of the unit.

Student Progress Information	Schedule for Updating	Possibilities
Online grade book	Weekly	An online grade book gives parents (and students) access to scores on daily work, quizzes, tests, and projects. This includes teacher comments on student performance.
Final grades for the quarter, semester, and year (or equivalent marking period)	Each grading period	This is part of an online grade book.
GPA and class ranking	Automated through the student information system	This information is of interest to some parents and students. The teacher does not have to enter this by hand; it should be imported from the school's student information system.

Student Progress Information	Schedule for Updating	Possibilities
Standardized test results	Automated through the student information system	These are of interest to some parents and students. The data should be linked to information on how to interpret the scores, and can be imported from the school's student information system.
Attendance records	Automated through the student information system	These are a good way for parents to check on students who may have attendance problems. The records can be imported from the school's student information system.

A Personal Aside

Indulge me for a moment by recounting a personal tale of parental frustration.

When my son Brady was in the fifth grade, he came home with a report card that was, shall we say, less than impressive. This bright, hardworking boy was getting D's in social studies, science, and health. The first parent-teacher conference of the year, which followed just after the distribution of the report card, was held ten weeks after school began, and it wasn't until then that I learned of the problems he was having.

At the conference, I asked his teacher a favor. "Please let me know what Brady needs to know in these areas, when the test dates are, and when the projects are due. I will help make sure he knows what he needs to know!"

A bit flustered, the teacher said she would get back to me.

I never saw the list of competencies or test dates, but I also noticed Brady never received less than a B in her class again. Although at the time I viewed this as a victory for proactive parenting, I have since worried that the skills and knowledge Brady should have gained during that year fell by the wayside.

Brady's teacher missed a tremendous opportunity by not enlisting my help and the help of the other children's parents. Over one-fourth of the year was gone before I knew my son was having problems. Even had I known he was struggling, I did not know enough about the curricular content or teacher's expectations to know how to help.

Parents do want to help. They just need information. And technology can help you provide that information.

Basic Productivity Tools

It's easy for anyone to get rapidly overwhelmed by the sheer number of computer programs available. The tools described in the following subsections are those that are standing the test of time and have proven to be valuable to teachers. (I've just realized I've been using a word processor for nearly thirty years!) The titles, features, and versions may change, but their basic function has not. Each tool is described with a short rationale for why teachers should master it, and each has an accompanying list of basic competencies needed to be considered a proficient user.

WORD PROCESSORS

The word processor, a program whose basic function is to allow users to input and manipulate text, consistently ranks as one of the most used computer tools for teachers. Microsoft Word has long been the standard word processor, but more and more teachers are using the word processor in Google Docs, OpenOffice.org, or Apple's Pages.

Teachers use word processors to do the following:

- Create instructional materials—worksheets, study guides, reading lists, and project guidelines
- Create tests, checklists, and rubrics
- Communicate with students, parents, other teachers, administrators, and the community through letters and newsletters
- Keep files of student records, learning plans, and assessments
- Write grants, curricula, and college class assignments

Nothing new here. Writing has always been a big part of a teacher's job. What has changed is that these materials are now easily modified, stored, and located; checked for grammar and spelling errors; read by all readers (not all handwriting is legible); and supplemented with helpful graphics and formatting.

One's work appears professional and can be easily shared among staff members (via flash drive, shared network folders, Web site, or e-mail attachment).

 Survival tip: When you've mastered the basic features of a word processor, you've gained many of the skills you need for using other tools that deal with text—blogs, wikis, desktop publishing programs, and e-mail.

A competent user of the word processor can . . .

1. Use the word processor for nearly all written professional work: memos, tests, worksheets, and home communication

2. Create a system of organizing, retrieving, and tracking revisions of documents

3. Edit a document using commands like "copy" and "paste," "find," "undo," and "save as"

4. Spell-check, and change the format of a document

5. Paginate, preview, and print documents

6. Create tables and insert graphics within documents

7. Create bulleted lists and numerical lists

8. Create a final product that looks professional

9. Save a file as a text or RTF document so people who use other word processors can open it

10. Take advantage of collaborative writing and editing environments when these are available

E-MAIL

The only tool used as often as the word processor is e-mail. Written messages, often supplemented with media, are sent using a program to others via a computer network, most often the Internet. Now a standard in business and in one's personal life, e-mail has both improved the timeliness of communication and made life more stressful with its implied urgency. Teachers use e-mail to do the following:

- *Communicate with colleagues.* Keeping in touch with colleagues, whether across the hall or across the world, is fast and efficient when messages are sent in the blink of an eye. Whether teachers are collaborating on a journal article, sharing practical experience, asking a question, or just commiserating about the state of education, e-mail is the standard means of communication.

- *Conduct school business.* Using e-mail for certain tasks is becoming standard operating procedure in schools. Once all teachers have networked computers on their desk, writing the school bulletin, sharing departmental information, reporting class attendance, collaborating on team-created materials, and communicating with parents can all be effectively done electronically.

- *Obtain information.* Educators soon find that there is a wealth of information that can be obtained using their e-mail accounts. Discussion lists, electronic magazines and journals, and daily quotes, jokes, and vocabulary words can keep readers current on almost any topic.

- *Create classroom activities.* As many classroom teachers get excited about how e-mail has provided them with new learning opportunities, they become anxious to get their students using this resource productively.

A competent e-mail user can ...

1. Identify and open the e-mail client (program)
2. Check and configure e-mail settings and understand how to use his or her username, e-mail address, and password
3. Identify each new e-mail message and determine its time and date, the e-mail address of the sender, and the subject of the message
4. Read and delete messages
5. Compose and send a properly formatted message and send a copy of a message to another recipient
6. Reply to a message, forward a message, and print a message
7. Create an e-mail address book
8. Create and use a group that sends e-mail messages to multiple e-mail addresses at one time
9. Create a signature file—and understand the elements of a good signature file, including alternative contact information
10. Organize and store sent and received messages and find older messages using a search tool
11. Quickly and accurately determine the importance of an e-mail message and recognize spam and phishing messages (those not sent by the person who owns the e-mail address)—and, of growing importance, to manage the settings of his or her own spam filter
12. Understand the rules governing the polite use of e-mail

WEB BROWSERS AND SEARCH ENGINES

Web browsers like Explorer, Safari, Firefox, Chrome, and their lesser-known cousins have done for the Internet what the Macintosh and Windows graphic interfaces did for operating systems: taken complex and confusing tasks and made them simple enough for everyone to use. This is a good thing because providing information in digital formats and accessing information using a network are increasingly becoming the standard way of doing business.

A good browser simply gives one access to the World Wide Web. It allows a user to enter a Web address (URL) to access a site. It allows the creation of bookmarks of specific Web sites so they can be easily accessed again and again.

Full-featured browsers are coming with built-in Web search engines to help locate information. And teachers increasingly access their e-mail, the student information system, productivity tools, and their personal documents through a browser.

The World Wide Web, of course, is a tremendous source of professional information, including

- Lesson plans, activities, and support materials, often designed and tested by teachers
- Links to online projects
- Professional research
- Educational journals and magazines
- State and local educational data
- News

There are many books and Web sites for teachers, students, and parents listing Internet resources.

Survival tip: Be sure to check the copyright dates of any book or the last date of updating of Web sites listing Web-based resources. Internet sites are often here today, gone tomorrow, or their Web addresses change.

Although lists of "preselected" Web resources are often helpful and time-saving, a good search engine and the skills to use it are even more valuable. Google is, of course, the biggest and most popular search engine at this time, but other search engines, often specifically tailored to a topic, can also be helpful. It's also important to remember that a lot of good information cannot be found using a standard search engine.

Survival tip: Check with your school librarian about the full-text databases to which you and your students have access. These are often a better source for credible resources than a simple search using Google.

Teachers can create bookmark "bibliographies" of curricular sources for their students: Web pages that include the addresses as links. Preselecting sites helps students get to useful and appropriate materials faster.

An extension of using Internet resources as classroom support materials involves moving the class itself onto the Web. High schools and colleges that are willing to become "virtual institutions" currently offer online classes and coursework.

A competent Web browser user can . . .

1. Understand what a Web browser does, identify the names of at least two popular browsers, and describe how to obtain recent versions of them

2. Configure the browser to open with a specific home page

3. Directly enter a Web address into the location bar

4. Use page links to navigate through the Web

5. Understand the functions of the toolbar items on the browser

6. Use "forward" and "back" buttons and a search history to navigate

7. Use a search engine to locate credible information on a topic

8. Print a page from the World Wide Web

9. Create and organize bookmarks

10. Explain and understand the district's Internet acceptable use policy

11. Understand what plug-ins and other helper apps do, know how to obtain them, and know how to install them

12. Understand the privacy risks associated with Internet use and how to minimize them by modifying browser settings

GRAPHICS AND DIGITAL IMAGE EDITING TOOLS

Today's students (or maybe all of us) are increasingly "visual learners." Teachers know that pictures are often worth more than a thousand words when trying to explain a difficult concept. Good graphic images in handouts or presentations should . . .

- Provide information
- Illustrate ideas and concepts in ways words alone cannot
- Create interest
- Help visual learners
- Provide memory aids
- Emphasize important ideas or concepts

Survival tip: Try creating a graphic flowchart of an assignment's instructions. More students complete the assignment and do a better job on it when this is provided.

Teachers use graphic tools to create professional-looking banners, newsletters, posters, bookmarks, name tags, signs, buttons, and certificates for a fraction of the cost of commercial ones. Graphics and photos in letters to parents can help pique parents' interest, thereby increasing the likelihood that the letters will be read.

Simple graphic tools are a part of most word processing and presentation programs. Clip art—premade cartoons and simple images—are a part of many programs and can be found in abundance on the Internet. (Check for copyright restrictions.) Lots of tools, like the venerable Print Shop, simplify the creation of banners, posters, and greeting cards. Special programs can easily help create time lines, flowcharts, and "mind maps." A host of "image generators" have sprung up on the Internet that help users create custom graphics with no artistic ability necessary. Being able to improve the quality of a digital photograph by cropping the image and adjusting its brightness, contrast, and color is essential.

A competent graphics user can . . .

1. Use both premade clip art and simple original graphics in word-processed documents and presentations

2. Place a graphic on a page or slide; change the location, size, and proportions of a graphic; rotate the graphic using the graphics handles; and align graphic objects

3. Distinguish between an image pasted in a document as an "in-line" text character and one inserted as a free-floating graphic, and understand and use text wrapping on a graphics object

4. Use the drawing tools within a word processor and slide show program

5. Use the clipboard function to take graphics from one application and use them in another

6. Import, edit, and use images from a digital camera in documents

7. Use a scanner to create digital images from paper documents

8. Use keyboard commands or a special program to capture a portion of a computer screen and save it as a graphic file

SPREADSHEETS

Spreadsheets are a practical way to keep, work with, and display numerical data in an organized, easily understood, and accurate way. Many "non-math" teachers (like me) find that spreadsheets take the drudgery out of calculations. Well-designed printed reports using data, graphs, and charts generated by the spreadsheet are rapidly understood and are, I think, more readily believed.

As education becomes ever more data driven, the ability to record, analyze, and use numerical data about individual students, such as test scores, is becoming a standard skill all teachers need. Spreadsheets can help all educators do this.

Most teachers are responsible for some budget keeping. Revenues and expenses are easily and accurately recorded using a simple spreadsheet. (You can catch your business office's mistakes.) Teachers can keep track of

- Fundraising sales
- Classroom materials budgets
- Departmental budgets
- Extracurricular activities budgets

Spreadsheets can be modified to create highly customized grade books if a grade book program is not a part of your student information system or is not supplied by your district.

You can make progress charts and checklists using a spreadsheet grid. Coaches and athletic directors use spreadsheets to record sports statistics. The results of any data-gathering projects, such as surveys, counts, or polls, can be organized and graphed.

A competent spreadsheet user can . . .

1. Understand the function of the spreadsheet
2. Open a new spreadsheet and identify rows, columns, and cells
3. Create a spreadsheet file with multiple spreadsheet pages and navigate among them
4. Use labels, values, and formulas in cells
5. Use a range of values within a formula
6. Add additional rows and columns to a spreadsheet
7. Alphabetize items in a spreadsheet and sort rows numerically
8. Format spreadsheet rows and columns by changing their width and height, format text in cells, and format numbers by places of decimal points and as currency
9. Create and size charts and graphs using the spreadsheet
10. Add spreadsheet charts and graphs to a word processing document or presentation
11. Select a print range

PRESENTATION SOFTWARE

Teachers use programs like PowerPoint and Keynote as presentation tools to accompany lectures and to create on-screen tutorials and lessons. The ease with which text, original graphics, clip art, photographs, sounds, animations, digitized movies, and Web sources can be combined to make multimedia slide shows a very powerful teaching tool for visual learners, enhancing the clarity of the information and increasing student attention.

Unfortunately, too many presentations are created that are simply long blocks of bullet points that may distract students rather than improve attention.

Survival tip: Think carefully about what information is best presented as a slide show and what might better be conveyed as a handout or Web page. (See the "Slide Show Cautions" sidebar.)

A competent user of presentation software can . . .

1. Understand the features, uses, advantages, and disadvantages of presentation programs like PowerPoint
2. Open a slide show in presentation mode, navigate through the presentation, and use the numbers on the keyboard to go directly to a specific slide
3. Create a new slide show file
4. Use the outline feature to organize the slide show
5. Select or create a background that appears on all slides
6. Add slides to a presentation and move them within the presentation
7. Add text, graphics, photographs, and sounds to slides
8. Embed video in a presentation
9. Create transitions (wipes, fades, sounds) between slides
10. Create links within the text or graphics on the slides to external resources, such as other presentations, other programs, or Internet sites
11. Understand some basic rules of graphic design that apply when designing a presentation
12. Use an LCD projector to display the presentation to a class

Slide Show Cautions

When I was a little boy growing up on the prairie, a big part of learning to shoot a gun was learning how to use it safely. I learned how to never point it at real people, how to carry it unloaded in the gun rack of the pickup, and how to hand the gun to someone else without either of us getting shot. Little things like that.

Unfortunately, most computer technology comes only with how-to instructions, rarely with how-to-do-it-safely instructions. Because slide shows that teachers make can be effective or ineffective teaching tools depending on how they are designed and used, here are a few slide show cautions:

1. **Have something to say.** Pretty pictures and lots of technology will never make up for a lack of interesting ideas and useable information. You can put all the pretty clothes on your dog you want, but he's still a dog.

2. **Organize it.** My English teacher taught me that in order to get a message across in a talk you have to tell the audience what you are going to tell them, tell them, and then tell them what you just told them. Good presenters use the outline function to put their talks together logically, and then use graphics, colors, or other on-screen guides to help the audience stay on track.

3. **Don't let the slides be the show.** The slide show should always be the second banana in any presentation. You, the human one, need to be the focus of the audience's attention. That means things like eye contact, enthusiasm, gestures, vocal variety, practice, and other basics of good public speaking are still as important as ever. Put the screen to the side of the room so you stay in the center. Use a remote so you can get closer to your audience. And PLEASE don't turn around to read the slides off the screen.

4. **Use a bright projector.** Poor projectors require a room to be very dark. Dark rooms induce sleep.

5. **Use good slide formatting techniques.** Poor overhead transparency techniques have carried over very nicely to computerized slide shows. Some very basic rules of thumb about slide formatting are as follows:
   - Never have more than five lines of text on a slide or more than five words in each line. Less is more.
   - Always have type sizes of at least 18 points for text and at least 36 points for headlines. Bigger is better.
   - Cute fonts are hard to read. Plain fonts are easy to read.
   - Use high-contrast colors and simple backgrounds. Make the message jump out.

6. **Don't go overboard on special effects.** Attention-getters like animated graphics, text that flies in, and strange noises really do get people's attention when used sparingly. But don't overdo it.

7. **Don't just use text.** We forget that many, many adults as well as children are primarily visual learners. And for all of us, a good graphic image can communicate a concept with more impact than can words alone. Most presentation programs can turn numbers into graphs and can import scanned examples of student work. Digital cameras allow us to quickly and easily show students and teachers in action. Short digital movies embedded in the slide show are fast becoming an expected staple of good presentations.

> **Survival tip:** When presenting to parents, peers, or the public, show pictures of your happy, productive students and you will increase the power of your message.

8. **Proofread.** Spelling errors in 48-point type projected three feet tall are much more embarrassing than spelling errors in 10-point type on a page. Remember that spell-checkers don't catch everything. There is an apocryphal story of a superintendent who welcomed back students and staff with a large banner that read, "WELCOME BACK TO ANYTOWN PUBIC SCHOOLS."

Please share these cautions with your students. There are many books dedicated to creating good presentations. Read one.

Basic Online Tools

Prior to about 2003 a teacher needed to be pretty tech-savvy to put information out on the Internet. You needed a mastery of a programming language like HTML to format pages. And you needed to know how to send HTML files to a server and to have the ability to get space on or maintain a personal Web server.

Web 2.0, a term that became popular around 2004, described a new set of tools and way of interacting with the Web. Thanks to these tools, which essentially allowed anyone who could fill out a blank form and click a "submit" button to publish information on free servers, it has become as easy to write to the Web as it is to read from the Web. Another common term for this phenomenon is the *Read-Write Web*.

This ability to easily write to the Web has created a far more participatory form of Internet use. You don't just read an online news story, you add comments about it. You don't just look at friends' photos in Flickr, you write compliments. When reading a professional blog, you may find that the dialog among readers following each post is often as informative as, or more informative than, the original piece. And Facebook has made our lives open for friends and bosses and parents to see and react to in a variety of ways. Have you "liked" someone's status lately? Web 2.0 has also provided the means for individuals to express ideas through writing, podcasts, and videos to an audience of millions—without the restriction of needing to have a publisher or agent.

Web 2.0 also allows you to control how much and when information comes to you. As all of us obtain more of our information online and less of our information from such traditional sources as newspapers, magazines, and television, tools to help find, sort, and organize news "feeds" have been created. We are also learning more easily from self-formed groups of peers online as well as from people who have become quite famous because of their insightful writing on personal blogs or through podcasts or videos.

Web 2.0 has also given teachers a new (and always evolving) set of tools to use to become more professionally productive. These no-cost or low-cost online resources, accessed through a Web browser by students, parents, colleagues, and the community, are relatively recent additions to the teacher's technology utility belt.

Survival tip: As you put both personal and professional information and opinions online, remember they will be seen by your school board, principal, parents, and students. We are increasingly judged by our online presence as much as by our physical one. Like it or not, Web 2.0 makes us all "public figures."

ONLINE PRODUCTIVITY SUITES

Google Docs and other programs like Microsoft Office 365 and Zoho offer a full set of productivity tools that are online rather than installed on your computer's hard drive. They can be used for the same purposes as the productivity tools described earlier in the chapter. Google Docs includes a word processor, spreadsheet program (with a nifty survey tool), presentation program, and drawing program. I've described the advantages of these cloud-based computer applications, and, in terms of skills, it's safe to say anyone who can use a regular word processor or spreadsheet will experience a very short learning curve with online productivity suites.

As of 2011, one enterprise solution adopted by school districts, Google Apps for Education, is being used by over ten million students and staff members at all levels of education. Google Apps for Education allows districts to maintain their own domain name for e-mail—a teacher's address is still MarySmith@anytownpublicschools.org instead of MarySmith@gmail.com—and gives access to specific tools to designated groups of users, such as staff or older students. In addition to Google Docs, schools have access to Gmail, Web page hosting, and a growing range of other Google resources including Blogger and Picasa Web.

But whether using a personal account or a school-based account, teachers will like the convenience and power of these online tools.

Survival tip: As you create online accounts for Web-based tools like the ones in this section, make a deliberate effort to record your username and password for each site and keep them in a safe place. Although sites usually have a means of helping users find this information, it's kind of a pain to recover it.

A competent user of an online productivity suite can . . .

1. Create a personal account or log into the district's start page to access the tools

2. Create new word processing, spreadsheet, presentation, and drawing documents

3. Edit documents

4. Save documents

5. Share documents and assign view-only, comment-only, and editing rights

6. Work collaboratively on documents

7. Upload documents created by desktop-based programs

8. Download documents that can be used by desktop-based programs

9. Delete documents

10. Create folders and labels for documents

11. Find stored documents using the search feature within the suite

12. Create and distribute forms

13. Create templates

14. Understand document revisions and how to use them

A Letter to Teachers About Google Apps for Education

This is a letter sent to all teachers in our school district about why our district implemented Google Apps for Education.

Dear Teachers:

This fall, all students in grades 3 through 12 will be supplied with Google Apps for Education accounts. Google Apps for Education is a set of online tools for communication, collaboration, time management, and document storage. Provided by Google to the district at no cost, these tools include

- Gmail: a fully functioning e-mail program and contacts database
- Calendar: a customizable calendar and to-do list
- Google Docs: a word processing, spreadsheet, presentation, and drawing program that allows multi-user access and editing

Google continues to add new tools, and the district will evaluate each for its educational potential. This is basically the same set of tools to which you as a teacher already have access.

As you know, all of these tools are housed on the Internet and can be accessed from any Internet-connected computer with a Web browser. No special software is required.

The district's primary reasons for supplying these tools to students are to do the following:

- Give our students practice in using current technology applications and tools, including e-mail, word processing, spreadsheet use, survey development, graphics use, and slide show creation
- Give students planning and time management tools and skills
- Facilitate "paperless" communication and the transfer of work between students and teachers
- Provide adequate long-term storage space for student work
- Help students work collaboratively, engage in peer editing of documents, and publish for a wider audience

There is also a cost savings for the district because fewer licenses for commercial copies of programs will need to be purchased and less file storage space needs to be maintained.

To ensure the safety of our students, Google Apps for Education student domains will be "closed." This means that students can only e-mail and share documents with you, their teachers, and other students within the district unless they specifically give others permission to view their documents. The applications also are spam filtering enabled.

Library media specialists will be reviewing our district's acceptable use policy and Internet safety guidelines when they introduce these tools to students. Using online tools responsibly will be an important part of the learning experience. (Please see the procedure that follows this letter, to be used if an inappropriate student use is suspected.)

We hope that you will take advantage of students' having access to Google Apps for Education by allowing assignments to be submitted electronically, using the program for collaborative work, and encouraging students to communicate with you electronically.

Please contact the library media specialist or me if you have questions about Google Apps for Education.

Sincerely,

Your Friendly Technology Director

Inappropriate Google Apps for Education Usage Procedure

The purpose of this document is to outline a procedure to be implemented if a student receives or creates inappropriate content within his or her Google Apps for Education account (in a document comment or e-mail). Student confidentiality will be protected throughout this process.

If a student or teacher discovers inappropriate content . . .

1. The person who has discovered the content reports it, either to the classroom teacher or other adult supervisor (in the case of a student) or to a colleague or supervisor (in the case of a teacher).

2. The supervising adult requests that the objectionable content **not** be deleted.

3. The supervising adult informs the library media specialist and building principal.

4. The library media specialist contacts the district technology director via e-mail, sending a screenshot and description of the offense along with the username of the student receiving or sending the inappropriate content.

5. The district technology director works to determine the source of the inappropriate content and reports to the building principal the outcome of the findings.

6. The building principal determines the consequences of the action if needed.

BLOGS

Blogs (Web logs) started as personal journals, often with highly political overtones. They have since become widely used as a means of both professional and personal publishing by a vast number of individuals for an equally vast number of purposes.

A blog in its most generic sense is a Web site that is updated on a regular basis; displays the content in reverse chronological order (newest entries first); and allows, even invites, reader response. A blog can be compared to a self-published newsletter or shared personal journal.

Teachers use blogs to easily create and share classroom newsletters and as a means for students to publish and share their own work. Many teachers have created professional blogs to share their work and ideas with others throughout the world, and many read other professional blogs to stay current on educational practices.

Survival tip: For students involved in research or a complex project, blogs can serve as a record of their process while completing the assignment. This information can be as valuable to the teacher as viewing the final project. Blogging encourages deeper exploration of ideas and concepts by the students throughout the course of any project. Blogs provide a great way for students to share ideas and discuss issues with peers.

Some popular blog hosting sites include Blogger, Wordpress, Edublogs, Class Blogmeister, and Kidblog.

A competent user of blogs can . . .

1. Create a blog for personal or classroom use
2. Add, edit, and remove a post
3. Add a graphic or photograph to a post
4. Use the blog settings to determine who can read and comment on the blog, and require that blog comments be approved before being publicly visible
5. Respond to and delete comments
6. Customize the appearance of the blog
7. Delete the blog
8. Find and follow blogs of professional value

A side note: as I wrote this book I shared pieces of it in draft versions on my own Blue Skunk Blog. The feedback I received from readers resulted in many improvements to the final product.

RSS FEED AGGREGATORS AND READERS

Following multiple blogs, news sources, and other regularly changing Web sites can be overwhelming. RSS feed aggregators allow you to create a single site that shows when Web sites have been updated.

RSS is a small piece of computer code programmed into a Web site. That Web site can then be tracked by an aggregator so the single aggregator page will show when the site has been changed. Google Reader is among the most popular and easy-to-use RSS feed aggregators.

In Google Reader, the sites to which you have subscribed appear in a column on the left-hand side of the screen. Sites that have new content are in bold print. One can either read the new content within the aggregator itself or click on a provided link to see the content on the original site. The new content can be "starred," making it easier to find for later reading.

Survival tip: iGoogle allows the user to create a single portal page that can be used to see many tools at one glance, including Google Reader, Gmail, Google Docs, Google Calendar, and more. It's my Web browser's home page.

Teachers can use RSS feed aggregators to easily find and read professional blogs, news items of interest, and current online sources of professional information by keyword. These handy tools mean the user needs to only visit a single Web page instead of checking dozens of Web sites to see if anything is new. Subscribing to student blogs that include an RSS feed and reading them in an aggregator help teachers track when these writing spaces have been updated.

Survival tip: The number of blogs one "follows" using an RSS feed aggregator can rapidly become overwhelming. Regularly unsubscribe from blogs that are of minimal interest or importance to you.

A competent user of an RSS feed aggregator can ...

1. Create an RSS feed aggregator account
2. Add a feed to a blog or news site
3. Read a blog entry within the aggregator and on the original site
4. Star an item and find the starred-items folder

5. Choose a "view" (expanded or list)
6. Create folders and place feeds into folders
7. View settings and manage subscriptions
8. Delete feeds by unsubscribing
9. Create a news search feed

WIKIS

Wikis are online tools that allow group editing of Web pages. Wikis can be one page, multiple pages, or as large as Wikipedia, the user-edited encyclopedia that rivals traditional encyclopedias for student use. Curriki is a project aimed at creating quality online instructional materials, supplementing or replacing textbooks, much as Wikipedia has replaced traditional encyclopedias to a large degree.

A table of contents on a wiki's first page can organize a large number of pages by providing links to other pages in the wiki. Links can be placed within pages to other pages as well. Wiki pages can include graphics, photos, and other media, including embedded video as well as text.

Although using wikis is one of the easiest ways to make information available on the Internet, wikis' real power comes from multiple people's being able to edit the content of the pages. The owner of the wiki site can give editing rights to specific individuals and groups or can open his or her wiki to the entire world. As changes are made on a wiki page, a new draft is created. Restoring a page to an earlier version can easily eliminate unwanted changes.

Teams of teachers are often tasked with producing material as a group. Whether you're putting together a curriculum, professional learning community norms, grade-level parent communications, or shared lesson plans, a wiki can simplify the creation process and give all team members an equal opportunity to contribute.

Popular wiki creation tools include Wikispaces, PBworks, and Wetpaint. Course management systems like Moodle often have built-in wiki tools.

Survival tip: Accounts on some wiki providers are free and without advertising if they are for educational purposes. Look for how to sign up for an education account.

A competent wiki user can …

1. Create a wiki
2. Edit the home page
3. Understand and use the editing icons on the toolbar

4. Add a link

5. Add a picture

6. Embed a movie

7. Add a new page to the wiki

8. Set up permissions to establish who can see and edit the wiki

9. Invite wiki members

10. Create a structure to organize multiple pages on the wiki

SOCIAL BOOKMARKING SITES

Social bookmarking sites, such as Delicious and Diigo, allow users to save their Internet bookmarks on the Web and create descriptive "tags" to help organize and find these resources.

The bookmarking site is "social" because it can be easily viewed by others (with specific bookmarks designated as private or public), or the entire bookmarking site itself can be selectively shared with individuals or groups. Because social bookmarking sites usually include RSS feeds, users can subscribe to other users' bookmarking sites to follow what they are finding to be of value. And, of course, others can subscribe to your bookmarking site to see what you add.

Bookmarks are classified by title, by tags, and by personal notes. A tag is a personally selected, single-word description of the content of the bookmarked Web site. For example, tags for a bookmark for a Web site about e-books might include: e-books, digitaltext, reading, Kindle, or e-texts. This simplifies the task of finding bookmarks on a particular topic because the site will show only those bookmarks with a specific tag when that tag is selected.

Social bookmarking sites will also generate a "word cloud"—a graphic in which the tags that are most used appear in larger or bolder type. It's an interesting way to analyze one's interests. (Word clouds created using a tool like Wordle are often used to visualize the topical content of things like political speeches and themes in writers' works.)

Teachers can use social bookmarking sites to make their saved bookmarks available from any computer and share them with their peers and students. Large numbers of Web resources can be organized by tags indicating the unit, class, or program to which they are relevant.

Survival tip: Use the "suggested" tags for Web sites provided by the social bookmarking site when you add a bookmark. It's an easy way to get started using tags.

A competent social bookmarking site user can . . .

1. Create an account
2. Add a bookmark manually or with a special helper application in a browser
3. Describe bookmarks, add tags, and edit the names of bookmarks if necessary
4. Determine how others have tagged bookmarks
5. Edit and delete bookmarks
6. Make a bookmark private
7. Find items bookmarked by others by using the bookmarking site's search engine
8. Create an RSS feed (search) for bookmarks on a topic
9. View tags as a list or word cloud
10. Import bookmarks stored on a browser

SITES FOR STORING AND SHARING MEDIA

There are dozens of Web 2.0 tools that allow teachers to store and share specific media on the Internet. Three popular sites are

- *SlideShare.* This site allows users to upload PowerPoint files and other slide shows so they can be viewed by others. Although some effects and embedded media, like movies, may not be a part of the converted presentation, users can view the slide shows directly from the Web site without downloading them or needing a specific application to open them.

- *TeacherTube.* This site works like YouTube, a video-sharing site, but it is meant for use only by teachers and students. Student video productions and teacher video tutorials can be stored, accessed, and viewed on this site. Many teachers feel more comfortable using TeacherTube because the site does not contain videos that are of little educational value or are inappropriate.

- *Flickr.* This is the granddaddy of digital photo-sharing sites. Users upload, organize, and share selected photographs and can find photographs shared by others. Many historical photographs from the Library of Congress's American Memory collections can be found on Flickr.

Survival tip: Students who miss a class can easily get caught up if you put your slide shows and video-recorded lessons on the Web.

Top Ten Social Learning and Educational Networking Competencies for K–12 Teachers

1. Knowing how to help students use educational networking tools to find information and communicate digitally with experts, peers, and instructors

2. Knowing the major Web 2.0 categories and tools that are useful in the K–12 setting and knowing which tools are provided and supported by one's school

3. Using educational networking sites to communicate with other teachers, students, and parents

4. Navigating, evaluating, and creating professional content on educational networking sites

5. Using online networking to create, maintain, and learn from a personal learning network

6. Knowing the district networking guidelines; following "netiquette"; conforming to ethical standards; and interacting appropriately with others, especially students, online

7. Understanding copyright, security, and privacy issues on social media sites and sharing these understandings with students and professional colleagues

8. Understanding the importance of identity and reputation management using social media and helping students understand the long-term impact of sharing personal information online

9. Creating and following a personal learning plan to stay informed about developing trends, tools, and applications of social media

10. Participating in the formulation of school and district policies and guidelines related to educational networking and social learning

Options for Sharing and Working Collaboratively on Documents

Technology designers are notorious for "accommodating" users by providing multiple means of doing a single task. (Open a file? Double click, right click, select it and go to the file menu, open it from within an application, drag it onto an application icon, or put it in the start menu—you choose.)

Choices can be good things as long as one has clear guidelines as to why one might select a specific option.

I am surprised by the number of choices many teachers have for sharing and collaborating on documents. The realization came to me when I started collaborating with staff wanting to work toward a less paper-full environment. Writing curricula, sharing staff handbooks, and working on building improvement plans are all seen as things that need to be shared and often require the input from a variety of individuals.

But sometimes it seems we are drowning in options and don't know where to start. Although the options may seem confusing at first, however, each method has characteristics that make it the right choice for the right purpose.

Ask yourself these questions:

- Is this creation something I want everyone to see, or just a few select people?

- Is there primarily a single author, or are there multiple authors?

- How complex does the formatting of the document need to be? How large is the document?

- How often does this work need to be changed or updated?

Use the following table to help you determine the right tool for the job.

Application	Advantages	Disadvantages
Create your documents in a desktop program like Microsoft Office, OpenOffice.org, Apple's iWork, and other computer-based tools and share them via e-mail.	Microsoft Office tools (Word, PowerPoint, Excel) are familiar to many and have extensive formatting options. The "track changes" tool can be helpful with editing and revisions.	Very large documents may not be sent via e-mail. Different versions of a document can become confusing. It may not be feasible to share documents with very large numbers of people. Only one person at a time can edit a document. Different writers may have different versions of the software, making it impossible for some to open documents. It's easy to forget to eliminate editorial comments from the final draft of a document.

Application	Advantages	Disadvantages
Create your documents in a desktop program and share them using a local network folder or a drop box on the school's student information system.	Documents are accessible to anyone who has access to the folder (or drop box), and access can be restricted. Sharing folders is good for large documents. Using and accessing shared folders may be familiar to most teachers.	Shared folders need to be created. Different versions of a document can become confusing. It is less feasible to share documents with large numbers of people. There is no concurrent editing of a document.
Create your documents using your school Web site's page creation functions.	Short documents are easy to produce using the simple text editor. Parents and students can easily access the documents. Materials can be created and changed quickly.	The simple editor is not good for longer, complex documents. There are limited editing tools. The printed copy may be formatted incorrectly. Coediting permissions may be difficult to set up.
Create your documents with online productivity tools (Google Docs, for example) and share them online.	These are simple tools that are easy to learn. Multiple authors can edit simultaneously. Owners can give view-only or editing rights to documents and limit access to them. Documents created in desktop programs can be imported and exported. Previous versions of documents can be accessed.	Documents are not stored on a school district server, which raises privacy and ownership concerns. Formatting tools are not as full-featured as desktop applications, so these tools are not as good for long, complex documents. Teachers must have a personal account or access to a school-provided account. These documents are not as easy to share with large groups or the general public.

Application	Advantages	Disadvantages
Create and share your documents using a wiki.	Wikis are easy to learn to use, and they have good editing tools. Pages can include embedded media. Individuals can use wikis to organize complex documents by creating a table of contents of links and through interpage linking. Owners can set view-only or editing rights down to the page level. Previous versions of documents can be accessed and restored.	The organization of such sites can be complicated. School-based wikis have to be set up and require administrative oversight.

 Survival tip: Make use of available privacy settings for all online accounts to protect your work and identity. How open you want to be will depend on the application you are using and how widely you want your work to be shared.

CHAPTER FOUR

The Technology Upgrade

The suggestion (or requirement) that one "integrate technology" into classroom instruction is sometimes met with resistance—resistance caused by the confusion and fear that come with doing something completely new. Too many educational leaders look at technology only as a means of "transforming" pedagogy—moving from those practices and activities with which we are practiced and comfortable to those that are radically different. It's little wonder we might resist.

Studies have shown that although a high percentage of teachers are using technology for administrative tasks, still only about half integrate computers into their daily curriculum. This is not surprising given that most administrative tasks are ones with which teachers are familiar, such as communicating with parents, recording grades, and doing attendance. A lack of technology resources, including computers, bandwidth, and staff development, may be an important cause of teachers' lack of enthusiasm, but familiarity with teaching using technology is a too-often-overlooked factor in determining whether a teacher uses technology for the purposes of instruction. After all, some of us went to school before there were personal computers or the Internet. (It was fun riding dinosaurs, however.)

The previous chapter was about how teachers can improve their performance using technology, but not with students in the classroom. This chapter describes how to move from increasing professional productivity to improving classroom activities and lessons with technology.

Getting Started with Technology in the Classroom

Constructivists say that you can't learn something for which you have no frame of reference. As a teacher, you can ease your way into integrating technology into your instructional practice by taking something you already do and adding a technology "upgrade."

In the table that follows, find some common activities that you may already be doing and some ways technology can be used to upgrade the learning process.

 Survival tip: Look for simple, basic technologies, such as spreadsheet software and presentation software, with which you and your students are already comfortable that can replace or enhance traditional activities and assignments.

Current Activity	Technology Upgrade	Benefits
Teacher lectures	Add a computer presentation program.	Graphics, sounds, movies, and photographs clearly illustrate concepts and heighten student interest. It is also easier for students to take notes.
Student writing	Require that writing be done using a word processor or desktop publishing program.	Students can easily edit and spell-check their work, and the final product will be handwriting-proof. Illustrations or graphics are easily added. Online peer review and commentary are possible.
Student research	Require that students use some online resources, such as an electronic encyclopedia, a full-text magazine database, or Web sites.	Information is quickly accessed. Notes can be copied and pasted into a rough draft. Sounds and pictures can be used in multimedia reports. Online citation tools make creating bibliographies easier. Having access to a large number of resources allows a topic's focus to be much narrower, making it more interesting.

Current Activity	Technology Upgrade	Benefits
Book reports	Use a spreadsheet or simple database with fields for title, author, publisher, date, genre, summary, and recommendation.	All students contribute to the spreadsheet or database. Concise reports can be used as a reader's advisory by future classes.
Math problems	Use a spreadsheet to set up basic math story problems.	Formulas and operations are clearly visible. A spreadsheet has charting and graphing capabilities. Data from original surveys can be converted into understandable information. Students practice numeracy rather than math facts.
Plays, skits, or debates	Video-record the presentations.	These can be recorded for later analysis, and for sharing with parents. Editing is possible. Recordings can be saved as examples for future classes.
Time lines	Use a dedicated time line creation tool like Timeliner, a mind-mapping tool like Inspiration, or a drawing program.	Time lines are quickly created and are easy to read. It is possible to add graphics and modify time segments.
Student speeches, student demonstrations, or student-taught lessons	Video-record presentations. Have students use multimedia, incorporating media into computerized presentations.	These can be recorded for later analysis, and for sharing with parents. Editing is possible. Save recordings as examples for future classes. Graphics, sounds, movies, and photographs can be used to more clearly illustrate concepts and increase audience attention. Slides can be used in place of notes.

Current Activity	Technology Upgrade	Benefits
Drawings or diagrams to illustrate concepts or writing	Use a drawing program.	Features of the drawing program can be used to create meaningful original illustrations or modify clip art. Digital camera images or scanned images can be edited and used with writing for improved meaning.
Class discussion	Create a class blog with discussion questions.	Students can contribute outside of class. Shy students might be more likely to contribute. Longer, more thoughtful responses may be given.
Games or simulations	Use computerized simulations, such as *SimCity*. Have students use online games to practice basic number facts, vocabulary words, or grammar.	Computers can provide realistic scenarios and visuals in simulations. Online drill and practice software gives immediate feedback and increases attention.

The key to a successful upgrade, of course, is the existence of a *genuine* benefit to using the technology—not just adding for its own sake.

Survival tip: Start using technology upgrades with activities that don't currently work very well: that poetry unit that nobody likes; the rocks and minerals unit that bores both you and your kids; the unit on converting fractions to decimals that leaves too many students confused. You have them—be honest. Even if things don't go exactly as planned, you won't be destroying already-effective methods if you start by upgrading the least-effective areas of your curriculum.

Based on the examples from the preceding table, some of the key benefits of the technology upgrade are

1. Helping the teacher address multiple learning styles by allowing extensive use of multimedia in lessons

2. Motivating reluctant students and students who are excited about technology

3. Allowing students to add elements of creativity, especially visual components, to their work

4. Allowing anytime, anyplace learning and access to information

5. Allowing student performance to be reviewed and critiqued more easily, both by the teacher and by the students themselves

6. Increasing the audience for student work

7. Increasing classroom participation by reticent students

An old adage suggests that the way to eat an elephant is one bite at a time. The technology upgrade can be that first nibble you take to successfully integrate technology into your classroom in positive ways.

Low-Hanging Fruit

Has your principal been after you to "integrate technology into your curriculum"? This seems to be something of an obsession in more than a few schools that have used the ready, fire, aim method of technology planning. "We purchased cool stuff, and now we need to use it!"

Overwhelmed by an increasing emphasis on test score improvement, ever-growing curricular objectives, and increasing class sizes, it's easy to see "technology integration" as just one more mandate from above. But it doesn't have to be that way if you as the classroom teacher use technology to meet some of the challenges you already have.

Here are a few simple ways to integrate technology into the curriculum that are fun, are educationally effective, and have a short learning curve.

1. **Digital cameras.** Good digital cameras, those with lots of megapixels, an optical zoom, an LCD preview display, and a PHD (Push Here, Dummy) mode, are now readily available for the cost of just a couple new textbooks. Every school library media center should have at least a few to check out to classrooms. Snap a picture, download it into your computer, and edit it with simple software.

   As a classroom teacher, you can use the pictures to add interest to multimedia presentations, school newsletters, and classroom Web pages. Kids can use digital photos to help explain science fair projects, record findings from field trips, document examples of geometric shapes, and illustrate their writings.

2. **Kid Pix, The Graph Club, and Kidspiration.** Each of these proven software packages for elementary students uses the computer in its most powerful form—letting students explore and create in a visual environment. Each is accompanied by a wealth of lesson plan suggestions. And, most important, kids love using them.

3. **Student Google jockeys.** As questions come up in classroom discussions, ask students to be Google jockeys who will find credible answers on the Internet using a search engine. Oh, and be sure to ask their reasons for believing an answer is trustworthy.

4. **Video cameras.** Video cameras are a powerful means of helping students improve their oral communication skills. Watching one's performance is always eye-opening and as powerful as receiving a teacher's critique.

Survival tip: Look around for old video cameras that use VHS tapes. These are easier to use than digital video cameras, and the tapes are simple to show, assuming you can find a VHS player and television.

5. **Collaborative writing tools.** Rather than passing handwritten or printed and word-processed copies of essays around the class, ask students to use a wiki or online productivity tool like Google Docs to share their writing. By the author's giving editing permission, other students (and you) can add comments that are easy to incorporate into the next draft.

The pragmatic reason for learning about and using technology may well be to meet a school mandate. But its use can make good pedagogical sense as well, increasing student motivation and enjoyment. Satisfy the bureaucrats and so something worthwhile.

It's a twofer!

Assessing Technology-Enhanced Student Work

As a teacher long ago, even before Steve Jobs and Steven Wozniak started working in the family garage on Apple, I required posters about independently read novels from my seventh-grade students.

It was a pretty good assignment, if for no other reason than that it provided materials for my classroom's bulletin boards that I didn't have to make myself.

When the posters came back, they were always of different levels of quality. Some looked like large sums of money were spent on glue and glitter and included a high degree of parental involvement. Others were obviously drawn rapidly on the bus or in the study hall earlier that day.

Although it was fairly simple to determine the amount of effort put into a given poster, it was not so easy to determine if the student actually read the book, if the student actually understood the book, or if the product showed any original insight into the book.

I lacked a means of determining the intellectual content of the project, and I never let the kids know what a "quality" poster looked like. My bad.

But on a personal, far more selfish level, I *had* discovered a great technique for getting a "quality" present for Christmas. I'd describe the hoped-for gift—precisely. By simply asking for a tie, heaven only knows what I'd receive. If I asked for a red and gray tie, my chances improved. But if I led my wife by the hand to the Jerry Garcia brand of ties at the local department store and went "ooh" and "ah" over one or two, I was pretty sure of getting something to my taste.

I reasoned, if I can describe a tie that I would like to receive from my wife, I should be able to describe a book poster or other product that I would like to receive from my students.

As you begin to work with students on projects that include technology elements that cannot be evaluated by standard paper-and-pencil tests, the ability to write an assessment instrument that clearly articulates the desired quality level of the technology skill or product becomes critical. Creating tools that describe what is expected of learners, whether in the form of a rubric, a checklist, or a benchmark, can help you dramatically improve your instruction. Of course this goes for things that don't require the use of technology as well, but the use of technology can add an extra element to your assessment.

Here are a few practical tips:

1. **Describe what you want in observable, concrete terms.**

   Remember the tie analogy? The more specific you can be with the indicators of quality, the easier it will be for students to determine the quality for themselves. A slide show presentation about a historical period might include a checklist of items to cover, such as

   - The location and the years
   - Proper clothing
   - Correct transportation
   - Tools and weapons
   - People doing their daily work
   - Key events (What happened that was so important that we're still studying it today?)
   - Main geographical features
   - Symbols (religious, job related, or holiday) that were important to the people in your region
   - Important or famous people, sayings, or documents

   Such a list makes it easy for both the teacher and the student to determine if important information has been included.

2. Create two strands for content and container.

Remember getting back English papers you'd written that had two grades: one for content and one for mechanics? Projects that use technology to help communicate the content really need two separate sets of assessment criteria—one for the content and one for the electronic "container" of that content. Whether the container is a video, a slide show, a word-processed document, a Web page, a spreadsheet, or a podcast, an assessment tool that describes the effective use of that container needs to be developed. Quality "container" criteria for the history slide show just mentioned might include

- A minimum of eight slides, each with a uniform background and layout
- Easily seen and understood navigation buttons
- A logical organization and structure for the stack
- Readable text
- Graphics, sounds, and movies used to add to the understanding of the topic

Survival tip: Clearly state what percentage of the final grade will be based on the technical aspects of the project. My advice is to never make it more than 25 percent. Ideas and information should be the most sought-after element of student work.

3. Use examples of past high-quality work.

By exploring past student work, students can see or read actual examples of quality. The critical elements, such as length of work, topics to be addressed, specific design criteria, and so on, need to be listed.

Survival tip: One of the dangers that using examples presents is that students may be tempted to copy the examples too closely. A way to prevent this is to change the assignment enough that this becomes impossible. If a research assignment looks at the attributes of effective leaders, one year ask students to choose scientists as subjects; the next year, social activists.

4. Give criteria to the learners at the time of making the assignment.

Assessment tools need to be shared with students at the time the assignment is given, not after it is completed. Students then have a road map to follow as they work on the project. The goal should be *no surprises*. Here is the task. Here are the quality indicators. Go to it.

5. **Use the assessment tool to help guide revisions.**

The term *assessment* has its roots in a Latin word that means "to sit down beside." One of the great philosophical differences between doing an assessment and doing an evaluation is that an assessment is a method that encourages continued growth rather than simply judging a completed task. The assessment tool should be able to help students see where they are strong and where they can improve. And by using the tool while the project is being completed rather than simply when it is completed, you can actively encourage such growth.

6. **Use multiple assessors.**

The best checklists I've seen have places for input from multiple sources. The teacher, of course, should comment on whether a quality indicator has been met, as should the student. The media specialist can add his or her own unique perspective. Parents should be given the opportunity to review with their children the progress of their work. And, in special cases, experts in either the subject of the research or the use of the media can provide insights unavailable elsewhere.

7. **Revise your tools each time they are used.**

No assessment instrument is perfect the first time it is used. Criteria can be unclear. Too many indicators might restrict creativity or originality. Find and eliminate all uses of comparatives and superlatives (*good, better, best*) in creating assessments. The terms are empty without precise descriptors of what actually makes something "better" than something only "good." Ask your students what parts of the assessment were clear and what parts were confusing. Assess your assessment tools and revise every year.

Survival tip: Keep your assessment tools in digital format, as word processing documents or database, for easy updating and reuse.

Writing good assessments takes time, practice, and thought. But the more experience we as educators get in articulating what we hope to get, the better chance we have of getting it.

Remember: *you'll only get what you want if you can describe what you want*. And that applies to both gift ties and student products. I've included a few examples of assessments for you to study, modify, and use.

Some Sample Assessments

Assessment Tool for a History Slide Show

Here is a simple example of an assessment of a multimedia presentation. Why multiple checkboxes? For a variety of reasons. The project may have multiple students or adults completing the assessment. The assessment may be done at multiple times during the completion of the project. The quality indicator may be described as "met," "partially met," or "not met." As you read through the criteria, ask yourself what's clear, what's confusing, and what might need to be added.

Assignment: You and your team are to research an early American colony or historical event (before 1770) and create a slide show to accompany your presentation to the class. Your slide show must meet the following criteria. Your grade will be based 50 percent on the content of your research, 25 percent on your live presentation, and 25 percent on your slide show.

Check off each item as you complete the items listed. After you have finished your slide show, indicate your event or colony and sign your names on the line provided.

Event or Colony:

_____

Your Names:

_____

Content

❑ ❑ ❑ **1.** In large, bold print, label your presentation with both the location and the years.

❑ ❑ ❑ **2.** Provide clues that locate your event in time. For example, show
- Proper clothing
- Correct transportation
- Tools and weapons
- People doing their daily work

❑ ❑ ❑ **3.** Include pictures of the key events. What happened in your area that was so important that we're still studying it today?

❑ ❑ ❑ **4.** Include pictures of the main geographical features:
- Rivers, oceans, lakes
- Forests, deserts
- Mountains, canyons, plains

❑ ❑ ❑ **5.** Include symbols that were important to the people in your region:
- Religious symbols
- Job-related symbols
- Celebration or holiday symbols

❑ ❑ ❑ **6.** Include important or famous people.

❑ ❑ ❑ **7.** Include important or famous sayings or documents.

❑ ❑ ❑ **8.** Provide the source of all information given.

Format

❑ ❑ ❑ **9.** Have a minimum of eight slides, each with a uniform background and layout style.

❑ ❑ ❑ **10.** Create easily seen and understood navigation buttons.

❑ ❑ ❑ **11.** Show how your information is organized on one slide.

❑ ❑ ❑ **12.** Use readable text and clear graphics.

❑ ❑ ❑ **13.** Add at least one sound or movie that increases the audience's understanding of the topic.

What quality criteria are missing from this assessment tool? Would you want good oral presentation skills to be demonstrated? If so, what might they be?

Survival tip: Don't hold students accountable for criteria that do not appear on your assessment tool. And don't expect some students to do more than the minimum, so make sure the minimum is enough.

Assessment Tool for a Graph

Performance checklists can be used with students of all ages. An assignment that asks a student to create a graph of the week's daily temperatures might look like this:

Assignment: Before you turn in your temperature graph, use the following checklist to make sure your work is complete and accurate. Attach this list to your finished graph.

Temperature graph for the week of _____

❑ **1.** My graph has a title.

❑ **2.** My grid is set up correctly with the temperatures on the left and dates on the bottom.

❑ **3.** The numbers on my graph are easy to read and evenly spaced.

❑ **4.** Points are plotted correctly on the grid.

❑ **5.** The temperatures are written correctly.

Survival tip: Ask students to create their own assessment criteria. What do they think will be the quality indicators of a good final product? The ability to assess one's own work is a critical, lifelong skill.

What IT Skills Should Teachers Expect of All Students?

Here is a modest proposal: schools should pick the top five information technology skills that classroom teachers should be able to expect of all students at each level of schooling (elementary, intermediate, middle school, and high school) and design short, authentic "tasks" that can easily determine if individual students have mastered each skill.

A paper-and-pencil test on IT skills seems shallow. A full-blown performance assessment would be a huge time commitment. A self-assessment rubric would be unreliable. But if a classroom teacher gives a task on and evaluates each skill at the beginning of the year, a profile of every student can be compiled and remediation can be provided through special classes taught by the library media specialist or technology integration specialist.

Here is what these skill evaluations might look like for entering high school students:

Skill Evaluations for Entering High School Students

Dear Student:

The expectation of this school is that you have some basic technology proficiencies in order to complete the work expected of you. These proficiencies include

1. Word processing

2. Spreadsheet use and graphing

3. Multimedia presentation software and digital image handling

4. E-mail use

5. Internet-enabled research

Each of these competencies is described in the following sections along with a required project and the assessment criteria that show mastery.

Word Processing

Expectations

I can use the word processor to complete assignments when requested: reports, essays, and other written work. I can compose a document in a word processor and edit it using commands like "copy" and "paste," "find," "undo," and "save as" to create multiple drafts. I can spell-check and change the format of a document. I can paginate, preview, and print my work. I can share my document with my teacher in a digital format.

I am able to perform the following tasks when using a word processor:

❑ **1.** Identify a word processing program and open a new word processing file

❑ **2.** Set preferences to show special formatting characters, such as spaces, carriage returns, and tabs

❑ **3.** Type in text and delete text by letter, word, sentence, and paragraph

❑ **4.** Insert text at the beginning, middle, and end of a document

❑ **5.** Cut and paste text; copy and paste text

❑ **6.** Use "select all" and "undo" commands

❑ **7.** Format text by changing font, size, and style

❑ **8.** Change paragraph justification and line spacing; change the margins of a document

❑ **9.** Use the program's spell-checker and thesaurus

❑ **10.** Create a footer that includes an automatic page number

❑ **11.** Preview a document and print the document

❑ **12.** Save a document under another name

❑ **13.** Save a document to a specific location

❑ **14.** Copy and paste text within documents

❑ **15.** Share the document with my teacher by e-mail, using a shared folder, or through Google Docs

If you have questions about any of these skills, please contact your library media specialist for help.

Assignment

Compose a five-hundred-word personal essay of three to five paragraphs on a topic of your choice (or as assigned by your teacher) using a word processor. Share the document with your teacher as an e-mail attachment, using a shared folder or through Google Docs.

Assessment Checklist

❑ **1.** The name of the file, along with your name, your teacher's name, and the class name and class period, are in the upper-left corner of the paper.

❑ **2.** A copy of the first paragraph is pasted at the bottom of the document, separated from the main text by several blank lines.

❑ **3.** The body of the paper is in 12-point Times New Roman font and is double-spaced. Each paragraph is indented five spaces using the "tab" function.

❑ **4.** The title of the paper is centered, in bold, and in 18-point Arial font.

❑ **5.** The paper has one-inch margins. One paragraph is formatted to have two-inch margins.

❑ **6.** At least one word is underlined that was flagged by the spell-checker and corrected.

❑ **7.** A word replaced using the thesaurus is in italics and bold.

❑ **8.** There is a page number in either the footer or the header.

Spreadsheet Use and Graphing

Expectations

I can use a spreadsheet for basic applications, such as keeping a budget, analyzing data, and creating charts and graphs. My spreadsheets include labels, formulas, and cell references. I can change the format of a spreadsheet by changing column width, row height, and text style.

I am able to perform the following tasks when using a spreadsheet:

❑ **1.** Understand the function and uses of the spreadsheet

❑ **2.** Open a new spreadsheet; identify rows, columns, and cells

❏ **3.** Understand and use labels, values, and formulas

❏ **4.** Use a range of values in a formula

❏ **5.** Add additional rows and columns; delete columns and rows

❏ **6.** Change the width of columns and the height of rows

❏ **7.** Format the content of cells, rows, and columns (for example, as numbers to a certain decimal point or as currency)

❏ **8.** Create a chart or graph using data in a spreadsheet with axes labeled or using a legend

❏ **9.** Select a print range

❏ **10.** Select a horizontal print orientation

Assignment

Create two spreadsheets to the following specifications:

A. Conduct an informal poll of at least ten of your classmates about an issue or preference (for example, their favorite drink at lunch, such as milk, water, a sports drink, or juice). Enter your data into a spreadsheet and use the data to create a bar graph or pie chart that is labeled.

B. Create a spreadsheet containing the following data for a class play that gives a running balance of profits or loss and calculates the number of tickets that need to be sold in order to break even.

Expenses

$1000 — Scripts and royalties

$500 — Sets and props

$300 — Costumes

$200 — Piano accompanist

$100 — Program printing

Income

$500 — Program advertisements

$300 — Donation from student activity funds

$5 per ticket sold

Assessment Checklist

❑ **1.** The name of the files, along with your name, your teacher's name, and the class name and class period, are in the upper-left corner of each document.

❑ **2.** Both spreadsheets have data clearly labeled.

❑ **3.** Both spreadsheets have columns of different widths.

❑ **4.** In Spreadsheet A, the following are true:
- Data are entered in the correct format (whole numbers, no decimal points).
- The graph is of the correct data and is clearly labeled.

❑ **5.** In Spreadsheet B, the following are true:
- Data are entered in the correct format (currency) and in the correct arrangement.
- A formula adding a range of numbers is used for totaling expenses and income.
- A formula to subtract expenses from income is used and labeled as "Balance."
- A formula multiplying the ticket price by tickets sold is used to calculate the expected income from ticket sales.

Multimedia Presentation Software and Digital Image Handling

Expectations

I can create a computer-generated slide show (a PowerPoint, Keynote, or Google Docs presentation) that can be used to accompany a presentation I would give in class. I know some basic rules of graphic design that apply when creating the presentation. My slide shows include images (clip art, original graphics, scanned images, and photographs) and text fields. The computer-generated slides help reinforce or amplify my spoken message.

I am able to perform the following tasks when creating a slide show:

❑ **1.** Explain the features, uses, advantages, and disadvantages of multimedia presentation programs and projects

❑ **2.** Create an original slide show file

❏ **3.** Use the outline feature of the program to organize the presentation

❏ **4.** Add slides to and delete slides from the presentation

❏ **5.** Select or create a background that appears on all slides

❏ **6.** Add titles, blocks of text, and bulleted text

❏ **7.** Add, resize, and move images to slides, including
- Original photographs
- Clip art
- Original graphics created using drawing tools
- Scanned images

Assignment

Create an original slide show of at least six slides on a single topic. The slide show must be organized, have a consistent style and format, and include both text and graphics. Submit a printout of the slides.

Assessment Checklist

❏ **1.** The name of the file, along with your name, your teacher's name, and the class name and class period, are on the first slide.

❏ **2.** There are at least six slides.

❏ **3.** All slides have readable text and a consistent format (background, font, layout).

❏ **4.** Each slide has a title.

❏ **5.** At least one slide has a block of text.

❏ **6.** At least one slide has bulleted text.

❏ **7.** Each slide is labeled, and the slide show contains each of the following:
- An original photograph
- A piece of clip art shown in three sizes at various locations on a single slide
- An original graphic created with the program's drawing tools
- A scanned image with the source clearly given

E-Mail Use

Expectations

I have an e-mail account that I use on a regular basis to communicate with teachers, other students, and people who might be considered experts in areas in which I am doing research. I know proper e-mail "netiquette" and safety precautions. I send, receive, and open e-mail attachments. I have an address book and signature file.

I am able to perform the following tasks when using e-mail:

❏ **1.** Access and open my school e-mail account

❏ **2.** Identify my e-mail username, mail server domain name, and password

❏ **3.** Check and configure e-mail settings

❏ **4.** Get new mail

❏ **5.** Open, read, and delete a message

❏ **6.** Send a message

❏ **7.** Reply to a message, forward a message, and print a message

❏ **8.** Create an address book

❏ **9.** Set up a mailing list

❏ **10.** Create a signature file

❏ **11.** Organize and store sent and received messages

❏ **12.** Send, receive, and open attachments

❏ **13.** Understand e-mail netiquette and safety, including
- Privacy issues
- Spam and spoofing
- Virus threats in attachments
- The importance of a signature file

Assignment

Send an e-mail to the teacher who gave you this assignment. Attach a word-processed document that answers the following questions:

❏ **1.** What does the concept "limited right to privacy" mean in school and business settings?

❏ **2.** What precautions should one take when opening an attachment and why?

❏ **3.** What do "spam" and "spoofing" mean, and how do you protect yourself from them?

❏ **4.** Should the same rules that apply to verbal harassment in school apply to e-mail? Why or why not?

Assessment Checklist

❏ **1.** Your name, your teacher's name, and the class name and class period are in the body of the e-mail message. The subject line of the message is "E-mail Assignment."

❏ **2.** The e-mail message includes a signature.

❏ **3.** The e-mail message includes text indicating that it has an attachment.

❏ **4.** The attached document adequately answers questions concerning safe and ethical use of e-mail.

Internet-Enabled Research

Expectations

I can use the Internet to efficiently locate information to answer my educational and personal questions. I know about and can locate information from the "free" Internet, full-text periodical databases, reference materials, and books located using online library catalogs. I have criteria by which I evaluate the reliability of the sources of information I find. I can properly cite electronic sources of information.

I am able to perform the following tasks when conducting Internet-enabled research:

❏ **1.** Effectively use an Internet browser

❏ **2.** Use directories and search engines to locate information on a topic

❑ **3.** Use the "advanced search" feature and term delimiters ("and," "not," quotation marks, and so on) to effectively locate information

❑ **4.** Know the subscription databases (reference materials and full-text magazine databases) available to me

❑ **5.** Use my school's and the region's online library catalogs to locate books

❑ **6.** Print or copy a selection of a page from the Web

❑ **7.** Know and understand the district's Internet acceptable use policy

❑ **8.** Use selection criteria to determine the reliability of information taken from Internet resources

Assignment

Submit a short paper that includes

❑ **1.** A word-processed bibliography of five information sources located by using the Internet to research a single topic of your choice (or assigned by the teacher). The bibliography, in the citation style required by your teacher, must include

- A magazine article accessed using a full-text magazine database
- An Internet site
- A book in your school library media center or local public library

❑ **2.** A paragraph copied from one of these sources, with a clear indication that this is copied material.

❑ **3.** A paragraph defending the authority of an Internet source you listed.

❑ **4.** A paragraph describing a search engine query using limiters to narrow the range of items found.

Assessment Checklist

❑ **1.** Your name, the name of the file, your teacher's name, and the class name and class period are included on the paper.

❑ **2.** The bibliography contains five sources of information, including
- A magazine article accessed using a full-text magazine database

- An Internet site
- A book in your school or local public library

❏ **3.** Each source is correctly cited.

❏ **4.** The paper includes a paragraph copied from an online source with a clear indication of its origin.

❏ **5.** The paper includes a short rationale for the authority of an Internet source.

❏ **6.** An example of using limiters with a search engine in conducting an Internet search is included in the paper.

Survival Skills for the Information Jungle

One technology upgrade that is common, practical, and, well, inevitable is employing technology to find and use information to complete research projects. Sending kids to print resources alone—books, magazines, and encyclopedias—just doesn't reflect the reality of information access in today's world. But this upgrade isn't as simple as it might appear on the surface. Why?

Research for most of us who finished our formal education prior to 1995 was conducted in an Information Desert. Those five or ten sources required for a research paper were tough to find in our school and public libraries. The final product of our information quest was usually a written compilation of information, often verging on plagiarism, to fulfill an assignment that neither requested nor encouraged creating new knowledge or finding innovative solutions to real problems.

Today's student who has access to online sources of information operates in an Information Jungle. A quick search using an Internet search engine can yield thousands of possible sources of information in a fraction of a second. Savvy teachers today are asking students not just to find and organize information but also to do so to answer genuine questions, offer original solutions to problems, and communicate their findings using a variety of media.

Although technology can be enriching, navigating the Information Jungle and undertaking projects that call for the demonstration of higher-level thinking skills contain perils as well. The role of the teacher has rapidly changed from one of a desert guide (helping learners locate scarce resources) to one of jungle guide (helping learners evaluate, select, and use resources of value). This change has been so rapid that many teachers have not had time to learn the skills necessary for their new role.

But for those who do learn these skills, the rewards for knowing how to effectively solve problems and answer questions in the Information Jungle can be tremendous.

Good information problem-solving activities and projects help teachers answer some loudly voiced critical questions:

- Is technology being used in meaningful ways in schools?
- How can we keep the curriculum from becoming "a mile wide and an inch deep"?
- Are schools preparing students to work in an information-based economy?

Teachers have been puttering with technology in schools for over two decades and don't have much evidence to show that its use has made a significant difference in student achievement. Programmed learning, drill and practice software, and computer simulations, although mainstays in many labs, have not resulted in gains in student test scores and rarely even attempt to engage students in more than low-level thinking skills.

One application of technology does live up to the exciting promises made by the technophiles, however: using networked computers with access to a wide range of online information as tools to support problem-based learning activities that help teach information literacy skills. Information found, conclusions drawn, and action or actions requested as a result of these activities can then be analyzed and shared using such business productivity tools as word processors, desktop publishing software, presentation programs, spreadsheets, databases, and video editing software.

So, what do the terms *problem-based learning* and *information literacy* actually mean? And, more important, how do they relate to the successful use of technology in the classroom?

PROBLEM-BASED LEARNING AND INFORMATION LITERACY

Problem-based learning is a constructivist approach to helping students learn essential skills through the actual application of those skills in answering questions or solving problems. In traditional methods of instruction, the teacher poses a question and provides an answer to the question, either directly or by directing the learner to a specific source for the answer (for example, "Read Chapter Twenty-Four and answer the questions at the end of it"). Using a problem-based approach to instruction, the teacher helps students answer genuine questions of personal relevance related to the topic: How does this current event have an impact on our community? Is there information in my health report from which my family can benefit? How can I apply what I have learned to my own life?

Why Use Problem-Based Learning?

One of my favorite units I taught as an elementary librarian was on H. W. Wilson's *Readers' Guide to Periodical Literature*. This useful guide was so complex that the company sold a complete package of materials designed to help students master its use: worksheets, overhead transparencies, and even a test about the material.

I used these materials to great effect. My students demonstrated that they could find magazine articles on a particular topic, identify the name and date of the magazine in which an article appeared, determine the author's name, and tell if the article included illustrations or graphs. I knew this because all my kids scored very, very well on the test that came with the teaching packet.

Only one question seemed to stump the majority of the fifth graders to whom I taught this unit. As I remember, it read, "Under what circumstances would you use the *Readers' Guide to Periodical Literature*?" But hey, they passed the test with flying colors, and I considered myself a pretty darned good teacher.

For students to be successful problem solvers, teachers need to teach what are commonly called information literacy skills. These skills usually include having the ability to . . .

1. Articulate the problem and identify the information needed to answer it
2. Know of information sources and locate relevant information
3. Select and evaluate the information in those sources
4. Organize, synthesize, and draw supported conclusions from the information
5. Communicate findings and conclusions to others
6. Evaluate the final product and how effective and efficient the process of completing the project was

Although many organizations, numerous states, and a variety of individuals have developed information problem-solving models, the Big6™ information problem-solving approach is one of the most popular in current use by teachers and librarians. Often information problem-solving skills are taught as part of an extended research project, but many teachers are also finding ways for students to practice a subset of those skills on a daily basis. (See the Everyday Information Problem Solving section in Chapter Five.)

INFORMATION PROBLEM SOLVING MEETS TECHNOLOGY

Most information problem-solving models were developed in the days of the Information Desert. Teaching students information skills primarily involved helping them locate books and magazine articles, compile and organize information from them, and write a properly cited research paper about a topic selected from a narrow list on which the teacher and librarian knew information could be found.

Happily many teachers and media specialists have found that information technologies complement and enrich information problem-solving opportunities. Students are freed from restricting their questioning to only topics on which the local library has materials and from communicating their findings only through written reports. Internet search engines and other online resources, such as full-text periodical databases, electronic encyclopedias, and content-specific databases, help make finding information on any topic of individual interest possible. Easy-to-use software, such as graphics, desktop publishing, and mind-mapping programs; wikis; spreadsheets; and blog and Web page creation programs, allow students to tell others what they have found using graphics and sound as well as verbally. Inexpensive video cameras, programs for editing digital video recordings, and places for posting finished videos such as YouTube and the school and district Web sites give students the opportunity to record their findings and share them with audiences outside the school. Exciting opportunities for involving students abound in the Information Jungle.

INFORMATION JUNGLE SURVIVAL SKILLS

Most jungles can be confusing and even dangerous to the inexperienced traveler. The sheer abundance of resources and multitude of paths to them demand that the explorer have special skills if these resources are to be used in constructive ways. Here are six Information Jungle survival skills for teachers and students.

Information Jungle Survival Skill 1: Know where you are going and make sure the trip's worthwhile.

How do your research questions stack up? Helping students prepare good questions to answer or problems to solve using information is more important than ever for a number of reasons:

1. The vast amount of information available makes research that tries to be exhaustive impossible for nearly every topic. Even in the Information Desert days students would often take a subject like World War II as their research topic. I would then show them the volumes already written on the subject and ask if they really wanted to rewrite all of that information. A clever way of helping students narrow the focus of their research is by helping them find a question, preferably of personal interest, about the broader topic. For the student who wants World War II as a topic, the teacher might ask, "What other interests do you have?" A student who expresses an interest in horses might then try to answer the question, "Did horses play a part in the battles of World War II?"

2. Plagiarism can only be avoided by having the learner ask genuine questions that require original higher-level thinking. Plagiarism has come of age on the Internet. Now when Mr. Fogy assigns a paper on the Olympics of Ancient Greece, the savvy student heads for a site on which a variety of papers are available for downloading on that topic. The "copy," "paste," "find," and "replace" commands used with an electronic encyclopedia and word processing program make quick work of a topic that does not ask for any original thought on the part of the writer. However, change Mr. Fogy's assignment to read, "How would your favorite athlete of today have done in the Olympics of Ancient Greece?" and the student now not only needs factual information but also must apply the higher-level thinking skills of analysis, synthesis, and evaluation—and those cannot be downloaded.

3. In order for all students to master information literacy skills, the problem or question must be of interest to the individual. Teachers who recognize the core knowledge to be gained through a problem-solving process understand that students can still make topic choices. If the purpose of an activity is to help students understand how the geography of a state affects its economy, it shouldn't make much difference to the teacher if the student looks at Florida, Nebraska, or Oregon. But it may make a big difference to the student who has a favorite state. Personal choice leads to intrinsic motivation.

Information Jungle Survival Skill 2: Learn to stay on the main trail to avoid the quicksand of irrelevant information.

Searching for information on the Internet is a pretty simple affair. Find a search engine like Google or Bing or Yahoo!, type a term in the search box, and find hundreds, if not thousands, of possible sources. Students need three different skills to help them improve the results of such searches:

1. They should learn to start with the best search engine. Google sorts results by interpreting the number of links to a page as an indicator of that page's value. It seems to work. Ask.com allows users to ask natural language questions—questions in the form of real sentences—such as "What is the population of Bolivia?" Students and adults should get to know one or two search engines well.

2. They should be able to use advanced search operators or advanced search pages in constructing a search. The more descriptive the term searched, the better the results. A search on "twins" will provide links to both siblings and the baseball team. Using the Boolean operator "not" ("twins not baseball") will cut down on the number of hits returned.

3. They should be able to discriminate hits that are relevant from those that are irrelevant. A child using a search engine to find information about "cougars" is as likely to find pages on sports teams, older women, and automobiles as

he or she is to find information on big cats. Most search engines return some descriptors that indicate the general topic of the page. Students need to read these and determine those relevant to their needs. This is true even when Internet filters are in place because students may search topics that might have sexual connotations.

By the way, another overlooked "skill" that needs to be reinforced is understanding that the Internet is not always the best place to look for information. A forty-five-minute Internet search for the populations of the five largest countries in South America can be done instead with a three-minute search in the library's current *World Almanac*—and with information that may be more accurate than that found online as well.

Information Jungle Survival Skill 3: Learn to tell the good berries from the bad berries.

Eleanor Jo (Joey) Rodger, former head of the Urban Library Council, once observed that libraries should have two large signs in them: the first hanging over the stacks that reads "Carefully selected by trained professionals," and the other hanging over the Internet terminals that reads "Whatever."

Even very young students can learn and should be learning to tell the bad information berries from the good ones. Because junior high students often make Web sites that *look* better than those of college professors, we teach students to . . .

- Look for the same information from multiple sources
- Look at the age of the page
- Look at the credentials of the author
- Look for unstated bias by the page author or sponsor

As students use research to solve problems about controversial social and ethical issues, the ability to evaluate and defend one's chosen source of information becomes very important.

A Range of Sources

Your students have been researching current diseases, and they come into the classroom with information from these sources. Could you help them determine which could be considered the most reliable? Might you as a teacher have a different opinion than some parents about the validity of information from some sources?

- Centers for Disease Control and Prevention Web site
- *Newsweek* magazine
- Best-selling book *The Hot Zone*

- Flyers from an insurance company or HMO
- Personal Web page
- Chat room conversation
- Rush Limbaugh's radio talk show
- National Public Radio's *Science Friday*

Information Jungle Survival Skill 4: Don't just gather sticks. Make something with them.

Traditional research assignments asked students to gather factual information and present it in an organized fashion. But if information problem-solving activities are to help students master critical-thinking skills, they must also require that learners

- Organize information to help determine its importance and spot trends
- Determine the importance of discrete pieces of data
- Anticipate critics of the findings or solutions and be able to defend their choices
- Offer conclusions and solutions that show insight and creativity
- Advocate an action or actions that can be taken by the audience of the research findings

This is how information problem-solving skills will be used throughout students' lives. Whether using information to select a community in which to live, a political candidate for whom to vote, or a camera to purchase, we gather sticks of information for the purpose of determining a course of action.

Information Jungle Survival Skill 5: Learn to play the jungle drums (and remember, others are listening).

One of technology's very best attributes is how much it can help us improve the communication process. Most technology curricula include how to use a word processor, desktop publishing software, spreadsheets, databases, presentation programs, and video cameras. Students are increasingly learning how to create Web pages and do digital editing. Learning such technologies simply for the sake of learning them leads to what some educators call "PowerPointlessness." Glitzy Web pages, noisy hypermedia presentations, or colorful brochures that are very short on content are too often the result of assignments that disregard content-area learning.

Using technology to communicate the findings of a problem-based activity keeps this from happening. The emphasis is not on the use of the technology but on the effectiveness of the information problem-solving process that includes communicating one's findings.

Technology has also made it possible for students to have a much wider audience looking at and reacting to the results of their projects. For example, findings reported on Web pages can be shared with students around the world as well as with family and community members. Broad audiences create students who are more conscientious about their work.

Information Jungle Survival Skill 6: Prepare for the next journey by learning from the last.

Information problem-solving skills are sufficiently complex that complete mastery of them is probably not possible. Assessment tools that help students continue to improve their information searching, evaluating, and communicating skills, rather than simple evaluative tools, are necessary. Checklists and rubrics that describe specific criteria for both content and technology mastery give students direction for continued improvement. (See the Assessing Technology-Enhanced Student Work section earlier in this chapter.)

THE HAZARDS ARE GREAT, BUT SO ARE THE REWARDS

Teachers who help students formulate and answer meaningful questions and solve real problems take chances. Critical thinking often leads to messy solutions, information literacy activities are tough to time, and higher-level thinking by students often leads to genuine intellectual challenges for the teacher. To be successful, teachers may need to collaborate with technologists, library media specialists, and assessment experts in order to design effective projects. And the results of such projects can be both spectacularly good and spectacularly bad.

But these teachers have the satisfaction of knowing that their students are using technology as a real-world application; that basic skills are being reinforced through their application; and that they are providing meaningful, motivational experiences for their students. And as one librarian put it, "The activities that require originality and creativity and the use of technology in order to solve a problem are just plain fun for both students and teachers." Getting students excited about learning powerful skills is the best reason of all for trekking in the Information Jungle.

Plus, your students will be practicing genuine 21st-century skills—which is what the next chapter is all about.

CHAPTER FIVE

Teaching 21st-Century Skills

The previous two chapters of this book have suggested how you as a teacher can improve your own professional productivity and improve traditional classroom practices with the judicious use of technology.

But we've all heard the rumblings that today's schools are not teaching the skills our students will need in tomorrow's technology-infused, global economy and society. Beyond the basics of reading, writing, and mathematics, what kinds of things will people need to be able to do?

The educational and popular press likes to use the phrase *21st-century skills,* but what does that actually mean? I can't predict the kinds of skills my grandchildren will need to thrive when they enter the workforce, and neither can anyone else—definitively.

But attempts have been made. These are three of the most popular sets of 21st-century skills being defined:

- International Society for Technology in Education's "NETS for Students"
- American Association of School Librarians's *Standards for the 21st-Century Learner*
- Partnership for 21st Century Skills's Framework for 21st Century Learning

Although these sets of standards have different organizational structures and emphases, they all recommend that schools should be helping all students master

1. Information literacy skills
2. Technology skills
3. Communication skills
4. Creativity
5. Problem-solving skills

6. Personal traits and habits that enhance lifelong learning abilities, like curiosity, tenacity, self-assessment, teamwork, and critical thinking

Survival tip: Check to see how your own national professional organization and your state may be defining 21st-century skills. Don't reinvent the wheel.

The Fourth R—Research

As painful as it sounds to add one more skill set to an overburdened curriculum, the case can easily be made that information literacy is as necessary a skill in the Information Age as the basic R's of Reading, wRiting, and aRithmetic have been in the past. What exactly is information literacy, and why write about it in a technology survival guide?

A simple definition of information literacy is "the ability to use information to solve problems and answer questions." In one sense, information literacy is a much-expanded term for the fourth R—plain old Research. Most models explain information literacy as a process, a series of steps, including

- Framing good questions about a topic
- Identifying needed information and the potential sources of that information
- Locating relevant data and identifying reliable information
- Synthesizing, organizing, and using the information to suggest a solution to a problem or to supply a defensible answer to a question
- Effectively communicating the findings using a variety of media
- Judging the effectiveness of both the project and the information-seeking process

With the flood of information now available through the Internet and an increasing tendency for people to use technology to locate, manipulate, and communicate information, I would argue that a better definition of information literacy may be "the ability to use information *and information technologies* to solve problems and answer questions."

The very glut of information has changed the nature of the fourth R. Here are just a few factors:

- **The increasing importance of the quality of the assignment.** A research paper that asks for a simple factual response can be easily downloaded from an online term paper mill.

- **Discretion in using and the ability to use both print and primary sources.** The preference of today's "Net Gen" students for digital sources of information may well leave them lacking skills for using print resources that add both authority and depth to the research.

- **The ability to choose and evaluate Web sites.** On today's Web, where middle school students can produce more professional-looking Web sites than can college professors, the ability to discriminate between accurate and inaccurate information becomes critical. If researching a health-related question, a poor choice of sources may be life threatening.

- **Development of ethical and safe online behaviors.** As students spend an increasing amount of time in the "virtual world," knowing how to treat others and how to protect themselves from the possibly harmful actions of others becomes critical. This one is tricky for teachers because we ourselves may be somewhat uncertain about what is right and wrong online. (See the Survival Skills for the Information Jungle section in the previous chapter.)

Survival tip: Consider information literacy activities to be a method of teaching rather than a separate part of the curriculum. For example, the textbook unit on weather can be replaced by a short research assignment instead. (Assignment: "Choose a potentially dangerous weather situation and recommend actions your family can take to guard against it.")

I've been happy to see teachers who have chosen to add information literacy projects to their weakest units, resulting in students' learning vital new skills and improving their retention of the subject matter.

How much attention are you giving the fourth R in your classroom?

Designing Technology-Enhanced Projects—the Four A's

Consider these scenarios:

Scenario 1

Mike is a wonderful young man. Handsome, intelligent, caring, and sweet, he's better than about 99 percent of the rest of kids out there. But the one thing he is not much of is a scholar. He is diligent, but perfunctory, about his school assignments.

On occasion, however, Mike gets very excited about his schoolwork. The period leading up to the science fair is one of those times. He spends weekends conducting experiments, visiting the library, searching Web sites, making graphs, taking photos, and carefully designing a presentation board illustrating his findings. He is involved, working entire days consumed by his task.

He completed one of his best projects in the fifth grade. He wanted to determine what substance, when applied to ice, would melt it the most quickly. He drilled holes in the bottoms of four or five aluminum pie plates, taped over the holes, and then filled them with water. After leaving the plates outside overnight, he removed the tape, carefully balanced the plates on measuring cups, spread a different material on top of the ice in each container, and then diligently recorded how much water dripped through the opening each hour during one bright, very cold Minnesota day.

He used his findings to design a spreadsheet and graphs on the computer. He researched facts about water, ice, and commercial de-icers. He used the information to verify his hypothesis. He practiced answering questions a science fair judge might ask. Not much here that could not be replicated by any student with some guidance.

Scenario 2

Ms. Jones's class chose an interesting way to examine the impact of World War II. Instead of having students read from a textbook, Ms. Jones asked for volunteers from the community to come in and be interviewed by teams of her eighth-grade students about what impact the war had on them, either as military personnel or as civilians.

After careful interviews, the students wrote narratives, took digital photographs, produced short video clips, and scanned memorabilia from the era. They looked for Web-based references to the topics and terms they heard about. And finally they used all this information to create Web pages, all linked to a single site, that allowed them to share what they learned about their neighbors. Students worked overtime to interview, write, clarify, rewrite, and design these pages.

At an open house, the interviewees and their families were invited in to view and comment on the students' Web pages. Over eleven thousand people viewed the Web site, including many distant family members of those interviewed.

For the past few years I have been looking at projects like these that both learners and teachers love—and that use technology and teach 21st-century skills. I've been asking students and teachers to describe learning activities they remember being particularly enjoyable. And in doing so, I have found that these activities shared many common characteristics.

These characteristics tend to group themselves into four categories. Each category is briefly described in the following subsections along with its implications for the development of 21st-century skills. Elements from the preceding scenarios will show what these characteristics look like in a real school setting.

THE FIRST A: ASSIGNMENTS

Assignments that matter . . .

1. **Have clarity of purpose and expectations.** Mike's teacher helped him and his classmates realize that understanding the scientific method, including how to form a hypothesis and how to collect supporting data through experimentation and research, was the primary purpose of the science fair. This is a lifelong, usable set of skills. Science fair students undertake projects worth doing, not just busywork.

Survival tip: Making sure students understand *why* something they need to learn is or will be important to them is probably the most important but most neglected part of a teacher's role. Unless you can convince students of the WIIFM (What's In It For Me) of the information or skill you are teaching, they will at best go through the motions.

2. **Give students choices.** Anyone who has ever attended a science fair has to marvel at the range of topics kids are interested in. Good projects surround every aspect of every branch of science, from chemistry to physics to biology.

Survival tip: Dig down and look at the core concepts your research assignments are trying to teach, and let the students pick a specific subject that interests them. If the purpose of the assignment is to teach a basic understanding of something (for example, the scientific method), it doesn't make any difference what the topic is.

3. **Are relevant to the student's life.** For today's students, World War II and the Trojan War both just seem "a long time ago." By asking her students to interview local residents, Ms. Jones added real faces and lives to history. The

stories resonated with those doing the interviewing. So many times we ask our students to research important topics—environmental issues, historical issues, health issues—but fail to help them make the vital connection of why the findings are important to them or to people they know. Relevant topics are always timely, local, and personal.

4. **Stress higher-level thinking skills and creativity.** Think how different the results of a science project are from a paper that simply asks an "about" question. "Hey, Mike, write a research paper about ice." Boring! Try instead: "Brainstorm an original theory, design a means of testing it, and find ways to effectively communicate your findings." Suddenly we've moved up on Bloom's taxonomy from the remembering and understanding levels right to applying, analyzing, evaluating, and creating.

5. **Answer real questions.** Mike didn't know at the beginning of his project what really would melt ice the best. His rather creative guess was that the laundry detergent (the kind with blue specks) would do the trick. The teacher may have guessed that there was a reason people paid for commercial de-icer, but the fact was, she probably didn't know either. It was interesting to watch as the experiment's data grew.

Ms. Jones had no way of knowing the stories the World War II vets would be telling. Their lives were as fresh and exciting to her as they were to her students. Unfortunately, teachers rarely ask questions to which they do not believe they know the answer. Sort of sad—diminishing to the student; boring for the teacher.

Try to Only Ask Students Questions to Which You Don't Know the Answer

Why do so many school "research" assignments fall flat? One big reason is that they don't ask students to answer an *authentic* question, only to supply a "right" answer.

A genuinely authentic question may have multiple right answers; no right answers; or no answers at all, only a conclusion that consists of more questions. Nobody knows at the outset of the assignment what the answer will be. The task should be a research assignment, not a fishing trip for predetermined outcomes.

During my training to lead Junior Great Books discussions many years ago, I encountered this statement: "Never ask a question to which you think you know the answer." The exemplar of an authentic question was, "Why, despite having a bag of gold coins and a goose that lays golden eggs, does Jack make a third trip up the beanstalk?" I'd still like to know the answer to this question.

Teachers, celebrate ambiguity in your teaching—there are very few right answers. And don't a few surprises in kids' work make teaching a whole lot more interesting?

THE SECOND A: ACTIVITIES

Activities that matter . . .

1. **Involve a variety of information-finding tasks.** As teachers, we are comfortable with our familiar old secondary sources of reference books, magazine indexes, and trade books. Yet the answers to many personal, local, and timely questions cannot be found in them. Secondary sources can provide excellent background information in the form of important facts, but often we need to talk to experts, conduct surveys, design experiments, or look at other kinds of primary sources to get precise information. The learners in the earlier scenarios spent time with secondary sources too, but the generation of new knowledge through hands-on experimentation and working with primary sources was motivating and helped students practice true 21st-century skills.

> **Survival tip:** Asking students to gather and use data from primary sources (interviews, surveys, experiments, real objects, and source documents) makes plagiarism nearly impossible.

2. **Are hands-on.** Mike's experiment involved using a hammer to pound nails, a camera to document his progress, a computer to generate and record his data and to make graphs, and scissors and paste to complete the poster board. Ms. Jones's students used tape recorders, scanners, digital cameras (still and video), and a Web page construction program.

   Students were learning by doing, not just by listening. Notice, too, how many corollary skills were practiced in these research projects: writing skills, interviewing skills, photography skills, layout and design skills, and speaking skills.

3. **Use technology.** Whether it is for planning, for research, or for communication, many students find the use of technology motivating. Neither Ms. Jones's students nor Mike used computer programs that were purposely designed to be "motivational." The challenge of designing containers makes good productivity tools, like graphic programs, desktop publishers, and Web page construction software, the virtual equivalent of a set of LEGOs. These are also the technologies students will be using long after they leave school, so they are developing lifelong skills.

> **Survival tip:** Simple technology skills that are applied to a real assignment are better remembered and more appreciated than sophisticated technology skills taught in isolation.

4. **Ask students to communicate more than just verbally.** Ms. Jones's students were asked to report their findings not only with words but also through sound and sight. Scanned artifacts like ration coupons, medals, and old photographs stimulated those students who might not be verbal learners. The stories told by the interviewees were captured and shared using audio and video files.

   Our ability to digitize and present information is no longer restricted to the written word; we now can include drawings, photos, sounds, music, animations, and movies. All are formats that carry important and often unique information.

5. **Are often complex, but are broken into manageable steps.** Mike's science fair project took him over sixty hours to complete and involved dozens of tasks. But early in the project he and his dad outlined the tasks to be done and established a timeline for their completion. Checking off completed tasks is satisfying and motivational, and Mike learned some planning and time management skills in the process. Large projects can be overwhelming, even for adults, but planning smaller steps, building timelines, creating frequent deadlines, and scheduling multiple conferences turn complexity into manageability.

Survival tip: If your school uses Google Apps for Education, students have access to online calendars and to-do list generators. Help students use these to successfully complete complex tasks by breaking them down into manageable parts and creating deadlines for each part. Ask students to share their calendars with you, the teacher, as well.

6. **Are collaborative.** Ms. Jones asked her students to work in small teams. Joint problem solving, assigning and accepting responsibility, and discovering and honoring individual talents helped create a synergy that resulted in better, more satisfying Web pages than those students working alone would have produced. Not every project needs to be collaborative, but real-world work environments increasingly stress teamwork. Working in teams on assignments not only is more enjoyable for many students but also leads to the application of practical interpersonal skills.

THE THIRD A: ASSESSMENT

Assessments that matter . . .

1. **Have results that are shared with people who care and respond.** Science fair participants don't get grades. In Mike's school, they don't even get any academic credit. Ms. Jones's kids got the same credit as those who took a

multiple-choice test on World War II. So why do kids go to all the extra work? Kids get hooked because big people take the time to really look at the work they have done and comment on it. Lots of other students all gather on science fair day and share their findings. People take the science fair seriously. The community, both physically and virtually, visited the students' World War II Web pages. Public assessments and reviews by peers, experts, and neighbors (any audience beyond the teacher) are common in scouting, athletics, dramatics, 4-H, and music activities and motivate students to higher levels of performance.

Survival tip: Want to see students' level of concern for the quality of their projects rise? Let them know that their final projects will be seen by other people whose opinions they value: parents, grandparents, peers, and the broader community. You don't really want your grandmother to see your misspellings, do you?

2. **Use authentic assessment tools.** Mike was evaluated on his science fair project using a rubric. This more closely resembles the criteria used in assessing a person's performance in the real world than does a multiple-choice test. Mike and his dad had the rubric at the beginning of the project and used it several times to check Mike's progress during completion of the project. It was easy to recognize what was good as well as what needed improvement. Quality indicators like rubrics and checklists that are given to students when an assignment is given can help guide learning and keep guesswork to a minimum. As students become more sophisticated in the research process, they should be expected to choose or design their own "rules of quality," one of the indicators of an intrinsically motivated person.

Example of a School Science Fair Judging Form

The following rubric will be used for scoring projects:

1. **Shows knowledge of the scientific method (oral presentation):**
   - ❏ 4 pts. Student explains all six criteria measured by this rubric easily; shows understanding of conclusion of the science fair project.
   - ❏ 3 pts. Student explains at least five criteria easily; shows understanding.
   - ❏ 2 pts. Student explains most criteria with help from the board.
   - ❏ 1 pt. Student tries to answer questions asked by the judge.

2. **Shows use of the scientific method through the project:**
   - ❑ 4 pts. Student presents steps of the method clearly and completely with headings.
   - ❑ 3 pts. Student presents each step of the method clearly.
   - ❑ 2 pts. Student has all steps on the board.
   - ❑ 1 pt. Student has some steps on the board.

3. **Shows enthusiasm and interest in the project:**
   - ❑ 4 pts. Student is excited about the project and eagerly tells about it.
   - ❑ 3 pts. Student is pleasant and shares information.
   - ❑ 2 pts. Student tells about the project, when asked.
   - ❑ 1 pt. Student answers some questions about the project.

4. **Speaks knowledgeably about the project:**
   - ❑ 4 pts. Student eagerly talks about many details of the experimentation.
   - ❑ 3 pts. Student shows understanding of the project.
   - ❑ 2 pts. Student knows what the project is, giving minimal explanation.
   - ❑ 1 pt. Student can answer questions when prompted.

5. **Presents scientific data in a well-organized, visually appealing display:**
   - ❑ 4 pts. Board shows data in clear tables, charts, or pictures with headings.
   - ❑ 3 pts. Board is neat and attractive, with limited tables, charts, or pictures.
   - ❑ 2 pts. Board has headings, with limited data under each heading.
   - ❑ 1 pt. Board has headings and limited information.

6. **Shows written evidence of research, experimentation, and analysis:**
   - ❑ 4 pts. Booklet has a cover, a table of contents, research data, interviews, a thank-you page, and a bibliography.
   - ❑ 3 pts. Booklet has a cover, a table of contents, and research data.
   - ❑ 2 pts. Booklet has a cover and some research data.
   - ❑ 1 pt. Booklet is minimal.

3. **Provide samples and examples that give the learner a clear idea of what quality work looks like.** Mike had a sample project to look at on the school's Web site. Ms. Jones's class in following years used the World War II Web site as an exemplar of a quality project. Assignments need to change enough from year to year so that copying is not possible.

4. **Allow learners to reflect on, revisit, revise, and improve their final projects.** Although Ms. Jones's class had a completion date, students continued to edit and revise their work as they received feedback from those they interviewed and Web site visitors. Learners get satisfaction from observing improvement in their work. Good projects, like gardens, musical repertoires, and relationships, are probably always works in progress.

So if we know all this about good projects, why don't all teachers design them with some or all of these elements? Well, a fourth A sneaks in: (teacher) Attitude is everything.

THE FOURTH A: ATTITUDE

Teachers who enjoy authentic, project-based learning . . .

1. **Are comfortable with a loss of control over time, the final product, and "correct" answers.** If some parts of the curriculum don't get "covered," if conflicting evidence causes confusion, or if a controversial solution to a problem is suggested, these teachers roll with the punches. They have the intellectual confidence to handle ambiguity.

2. **Accept active students rather than passive students.** These teachers have developed new rules of behavior that stress student responsibility, and have trained their principals to differentiate between active learning and a classroom out of control.

3. **Believe that given enough time, resources, and motivation, all students are capable of high performance.** It's not just the talented and gifted students who can make choices, solve problems creatively, and complete complex tasks. These teachers know that most students rise to the level of performance expected of them and that great ideas can come from anyone in the class.

4. **Recognize that their expertise must be in the learning and research process, not just in a subject area.** No longer are these teachers just information dispensers—they are guides for information-building students. The happiest teachers are colearners in the classroom, especially when learning new technology tools. Students get the satisfaction that comes from teaching as well.

5. **Know that their own enthusiasm is more important than ever.** The best projects I have seen have always been designed by teachers who are enthusiastic about what they are doing and how they are doing it. The downside to this is that it is very difficult to create recipes for or give examples

of specific projects that can be easily adopted by other teachers. No project, no matter how well designed, is going to work for every teacher and every group of students.

However, we can all take principles and guidelines like the ones in this chapter and apply them to the individual subjects about which we, ourselves, are passionate. And that passion will be contagious.

6. **Understand that these kinds of projects don't always work the first time.** But they keep trying.

Projects must matter. The research needs to be important to the student. If it isn't, students will only go through the motions.

Survival tip: Students inherently understand that *a job not worth doing is not worth doing well.*

One of the best things we as teachers can do is work very hard to make sure projects are well designed and intrinsically motivating. Compare your next assignment to the following rubric. Aim for level three in all your projects, and hope your students are lucky enough to get to do a few level-four tasks sometime during their school years.

Research Question Rubric: Not All Research Questions Are Created Equal

Level One

My research is about a broad topic. I can complete the assignment by using a general reference source, such as an encyclopedia. I have no personal questions about the topic.

Primary example: My research is about an animal.

Secondary example: My research is about the economy of a state.

Level Two

My research answers a question that helps me narrow the focus of my information gathering. This question may mean that I need to go to various sources to get enough information to create a reliable answer. The conclusion of the research will ask me to give a supported answer to the question.

> *Primary example:* What methods has my animal developed to help it survive?
>
> *Secondary example:* What role has manufacturing played in a state's economic development?

Level Three

My research answers a question of personal relevance. To answer this question I may need not just to consult secondary sources, such as magazines, newspapers, books, or the Internet, but also to use primary sources of information, such as original surveys, interviews, or source documents.

> *Primary example:* Would my animal be a good choice for my family to adopt as a pet?
>
> *Secondary example:* How can one best prepare for a career in manufacturing in my area?

Level Four

My research answers a personal question about the topic, and it contains information that may be of use to decision makers as they develop policies or distribute funds. The result of my research is a well-supported and creative conclusion that contains a call for action on the part of an organization or government body. I have a plan to distribute this information.

> *Primary example:* How can our school help preserve the environment in which my animal lives?
>
> *Secondary example:* How might my high school change its curricula to meet the needs of students wanting a career in manufacturing?

Enjoyable learning experiences that are both motivating and meaningful don't just happen. They require thoughtful preparation and the conscious use of "lessons learned" from previous successful projects. All of us who work with students on research projects need to keep asking ourselves questions like the following:

1. What are the barriers to better research?

2. How do we create meaningful assessment tools that can help us become more comfortable with ambiguity?

3. How do I make sure every student is intrinsically motivated to keep learning throughout his or her life by finding, evaluating, and using information?

4. How do information technologies both help with and detract from good information problem solving?

21st-century skills are a reality that all of us, students and teachers alike, need to master.

Everyday Information Problem Solving

When we base our information problem-solving instruction around a single giant unit or two each year, students forget all these important defining, locating, accessing, synthesizing, communicating, and evaluating skills because of the lack of opportunity to practice. That's why we seem to reteach the use of the library catalog, search engines, Web site evaluation strategies, online periodical databases, and even word processing commands year after year to the same group of students who once seemed to have grasped them.

Practicing information problem solving needs to be a daily activity for every student in our schools, not just a biennial "event."

It's easy to quickly brainstorm a whole raft of information problem-solving mini-activities that can be done right in the classroom using the Internet:

- Check the local weather forecast and make a recommendation about dress for the next day.

- Search for and report an interesting fact about the author of the next story being read by the class.

- E-mail students in another class to ask their opinions on a discussion topic.

- Recommend a movie or television show to watch the coming weekend using a critic's advice.

- Find two science articles that relate to the current science unit. Evaluate the credibility of the sources of information.

- Locate a place from a current news headline or class reading on an online map resource.
- Recommend a book to a classmate based on other books that classmate has read using the school's library catalog or an Internet source.
- Update the class Web page with interesting facts from units studied and links to related information on the Web.
- Estimate the number of calories and grams of fat in the meal served in the cafeteria that day.
- Find a "quote of the day" on a specific topic and use a graphics program to illustrate it and print it out.
- Video-record a short demonstration or verbal report done by a student.

Note that most of these tasks take fewer than ten or fifteen minutes for a skilled information searcher to complete. Each has direct relevance to the student's academic or personal life. Reporting the results of the research is informal and interesting. Most of these activities are meaningful ones that adults do as well.

Entertain or Engage? Why You Need to Know the Difference

Teachers lament that given the amount of time kids are spending online, they now must be entertained if you want their attention. It's not an uncommon complaint. I hear it often when I ask teachers to list some qualities of today's students.

But I don't believe it is a valid observation. The terms *entertain* and *engage* are being confused. There are important distinctions. The definitions of these words, adapted from the Merriam-Webster online dictionary, hint at the difference:

> **Engage:** to hold the attention of; to induce to participate
>
> **Entertain:** to provide entertainment (amusement or diversion provided especially by performers)

In learning environments, entertainment and engagement look quite different, and it's easy to tell them apart:

Entertainment	Engagement
Entertainment's primary purpose is to create an enjoyable experience.	Engagement's primary purpose is to focus attention so learning occurs.
Entertainment is ephemeral and often frivolous.	Engagement creates long-lasting results and deals with important issues.

Entertainment	Engagement
Entertainment needs have little relevance to the reader/watcher/listener.	Engagement involves experiences that are personal, topical, or local.
Entertainment is an escape from problems (or when problems are a part of entertainment, the clever solutions are given).	Engagement involves solving problems, and the learner supplies the solutions.
Entertainment results from the creativity of people other than the learner.	Engagement asks for creativity on the part of the learner.
Entertainment is often passive.	Engagement is active or interactive.

I am not convinced that today's kids need constant entertainment any more or less than any of us do. But they are more insistent on learning that is engaging.

When today's children disappear for hours on end, it is often not to watch television (a passive form of entertainment) but to play video games, chat, and interact with Internet sites (active forms of engagement).

Remember that there *is* a difference between entertaining and engaging the learner. We all need to make the distinction. And we need to make engagement the focus of our instructional strategy improvements. Today's students *are* more demanding, but we need to ask ourselves carefully what they are really insisting on in their classrooms.

Why Robots Make the Best Students

- They don't challenge the teacher's authority or subject expertise.
- They don't ask questions that might not have a right or wrong answer.
- They all learn in the same way, at the same pace.
- They stay in their seat with their eyes straight ahead.
- They don't go on vacations with their families during school time or skip school.
- They don't need to learn to work in cooperative groups. Or need social skills. Or need conflict resolution abilities.
- They don't need sex education, multicultural education, or physical education. The arts and literature are wasted on them. No field trips, no fire drills, no hot lunch.

- They never make the principal or teacher look bad (for example, stupid, incompetent, clueless . . .).
- They follow the school dress code and never swear.
- They have no strongly held opinions or passions for which to fight.
- They always pass the state tests, and they all read at grade level.
- They are always willing to do the homework no matter how meaningless.
- They don't complain when lectured or given worksheets. Endlessly.
- They can all use the same textbook, and they are all always on the same chapter.
- They make good robot employees.

A Few Thoughts About Creativity

Quite a number of "21st-century skill" lists include creativity as one of those abilities tomorrow's most productive workers will need to possess.

We in education are supposed to be producing creative graduates. It's something we as educators give a good deal of lip service to and like to think we encourage in students—but only to a degree. Too much creativity makes us a little nervous, and the student who is less creative is also less challenging. (See the "Why Robots Make the Best Students" sidebar.)

I have some thoughts about *creativity,* as the term is commonly used in schools, and teaching, and technology.

Creativity isn't always about art. I tend to appreciate creative problem solvers as much as, or more than, I appreciate those folks who are creative in a more "artistic" fashion. Or maybe we need to extend the definition of "art" to dealing with people and situations in new and effective ways. The creativity I admire most, especially in my staff, involves simply figuring out a way of accomplishing a task in a better way or dealing effectively with a problem—mechanical or human. I hope we never narrow what constitutes a creative endeavor.

What are some ways in which human beings demonstrate creativity?

- As writers, presenters, and storytellers
- As mathematicians
- As graphic artists (through drawing, painting, sculpting, photographing, and designing)
- As athletes and dancers, kinetically
- As musicians

- As humorists
- As team builders and collaborators
- As problem solvers
- As inventors
- As leaders who organize, motivate, and inspire

Are we restricting creativity to the art room and creative writing class when it should be in *every* class, unit, and activity?

Creativity must be accompanied by craft and discipline. When most of us look at a Jackson Pollock painting, we usually think something like, "Gee whiz, give (a) a monkey, (b) a little kid, or (c) me a can of paint and I can make a painting like that." We'd be wrong. Even abstract artists understand balance and tone, and they exhibit just plain great craftsmanship and technical skills. The most original written ideas in the world are inaccessible when locked behind faulty grammar, spelling, syntax, or organization. Digital music composition programs like GarageBand will not cure a tin ear.

Too many students think that sufficient creativity will overcome a lack of skill or circumvent the need for discipline or practice. Creativity unaccompanied by drive, self-discipline, or just hard work and practice isn't worth much. Do we ask students to be both creative *and* disciplined?

If we ask students to demonstrate creativity or innovation, we need some tools to determine whether they have done so successfully. Like with pornography, I don't think I can define creativity, but I think I know it when I see it. But that won't cut it in the assessment world. As much as I admire those who advocate 21st-century skills for including creativity as one of their student technology skill standards, I am not sure it is fair to hold students accountable for mastering it if we can't describe what it looks like, provide models, and somewhat objectively determine whether a student has been creative.

As educators, we really don't know much about creativity. Some of the myths about creativity in the business environment that Teresa Amabile at the Harvard Business School (Breen, 2004) has discovered include the following (with counterpoints in parentheses):

- Creativity only comes from "creative" people. (Everyone can be creative.)
- Creativity is motivated by rewards. (People would prefer to engage deeply in their work and see progress.)
- Competition spurs creativity. (Teams that share and debate ideas are more creative.)

There were surprises here for me. I know I have a lot more to learn about enhancing and supporting creativity in education. Are any teacher-training efforts being diverted from "raising test scores" to "thinking outside the quadrilateral parallelogram"?

Think creatively about creativity in your classroom.

Right-Brain Skills and Technology: A Whole New Mind(-Set)

Thomas Friedman's book *The World is Flat* and its report on the rise of white-collar job outsourcing to foreign labor markets scared me. But Daniel Pink's wonderful book *A Whole New Mind: Moving from the Information Age to the Conceptual Age* (2006) brings some relief—if not a little optimism. There *will* be a place for our kids in tomorrow's workplace, assuming, of course, that teachers take some lessons from the book. A big assumption.

Like Friedman, Pink acknowledges the labor-outsourcing trend. He also describes two other economic factors that will have an impact on the kinds of skills future workers will need: abundance and automation. He suggests that readers ask themselves three questions about their job (p. 245):

1. Can someone overseas do it cheaper?

2. Can a computer do it faster?

3. Am I offering something that satisfies the nonmaterial, transcendent desires of an abundant age? [Am I making not just products, but products that satisfy the user's aesthetic sensibilities?]

Pink believes that as a result of these trends we are shifting from the Information Age to the Conceptual Age, and that "right-brainers will rule the future." Successful players in this new economy will increasingly be required to develop and use the right-brain abilities of high-level conceptualization (seeing the larger picture, synthesizing information) and high-touch sensibilities (being empathetic, creating meaning). Happy news, perhaps, for those of us who never were all that good at the left-brain stuff in the first place.

More specifically, Pink suggests we work toward developing in ourselves (and, by implication, our students), six right-brain "senses" to complement our left-brain analytical skills.

In the age of educational accountability, too many classrooms seem to be gearing all their instructional efforts toward helping students master left-brain skills because these are what standardized tests measure. But to what extent as teachers *do* we develop and *should* we also be developing right-brain skills?

Using Pink's six observations that follow (2010, pp. 65–66), might teachers cultivate the skills needed by the workers of the Conceptual Age with the help of technology?

1. **Not just function, but also DESIGN.** "It's no longer sufficient to create a product, a service, an experience, or a lifestyle that's merely functional. Today it's economically crucial and personally rewarding to create something that is also beautiful, whimsical, or emotionally engaging."

   Technology can help teachers . . .

   - Provide students with access to e-picture books and graphic novels, along with Web sites about illustrators and their work

   - Assess not only the content but also the appearance of student work

   - Build visual literacy

   - Emphasize design principles as part of desktop publishing, creating multimedia presentations, and Web page development

2. **Not just argument, but also STORY.** "When our lives are brimming with information and data, it's not enough to marshal an effective argument. . . . The essence of persuasion, communication, and self-understanding has become the ability also to fashion a compelling story."

   Technology can help teachers . . .

   - Encourage students to complement speaking skills with multimedia presentations

   - Give students opportunities to both hear and tell stories in a digital format

3. **Not just focus, but also SYMPHONY.** "What's in greatest demand today isn't analysis but synthesis—seeing the big picture and, crossing boundaries, being able to combine disparate pieces into an arresting new whole."

   Technology can help teachers . . .

   - Design classroom projects that cross disciplines

   - Help students apply technology skills and concepts to genuine problems

   - Provide multiple sources of digital and print information for research or information literacy activities

4. **Not just logic, but also EMPATHY.** "What will distinguish those who thrive will be their ability to understand what makes their fellow woman or man tick, to forge relationships, and to care for others."

   Technology can help teachers . . .

   - Provide students with online materials about people from other cultures and socioeconomic groups

   - Plan and conduct group projects that involve students in schools in other countries

5. **Not just seriousness, but also PLAY**. "Ample evidence points to the enormous health and professional benefits of laughter, lightheartedness, games, and humor."

    Technology can help teachers . . .

    - Provide access to online games
    - Allow students to use digital storytelling techniques that require action and music
    - Provide access to riddles and jokes, and encourage students to create their own, tell them, and share them online

6. **Not just accumulation, but also MEANING.** "[Material plenty] has freed hundreds of millions of people from day-to-day struggles and liberated us to pursue more significant desires: purpose, transcendence, and spiritual fulfillment."

    Technology can help teachers . . .

    - Provide access to stories from different religions, myths, and legends
    - Infuse lessons about ethical technology behaviors as a part of every project
    - Create projects that include statements of personal values

    I will also be bold enough to add a seventh "sense" of my own to Pink's list:

7. **Not just knowledge, but also LEARNING.** Unless a person develops both the ability and the desire to continue to learn new skills; to be open to new ideas; and to be ready to change practices in the face of new technologies, economic forces, and societal demands, he or she will not be able to successfully compete in a global economy.

    Technology can help teachers . . .

    - Create projects that stress processes, not just facts
    - Encourage students to research areas of personal interest (and tolerate a diversity of interests) online
    - Encourage students to learn in nontraditional ways (online, through early enrollment in college, or through e-mentoring), and support students in such learning environments

Are you surprised to see how many of these right-brain senses you are already expanding, with or without technology? Good teachers have always strived for balance.

Our society and educational system sadly see many of the opportunities just listed as "extras"—frills that are often the first to be cut in times of tight budgets. We are doing a disservice to our students as future workers and citizens by doing so.

I Will as a Teacher . . .

Let's hold a little friendly competition between using technology as a part of your pedagogical toolbox versus pretending it doesn't exist:

- "I will provide up-to-date information to my students" versus "I have a textbook that is five years old."

- "I will find and change all my instructional materials, worksheets, study guides, and tests every year" versus "I hope the master is good enough for one more photocopy."

- "I will model 21st-century skills (using technology, information problem solving, and lifelong learning)" versus "I will lecture about them."

- "I will provide my visual learners with an accessible means of grasping concepts through multimedia resources" versus "I can use simpler words and speak more slowly."

- "I will give my students a worldwide audience for their creative work" versus "I sometimes share my students' work with the rest of the class."

- "I will give my students access to study materials and resources online 24/7" versus "I hope they remember to bring home the textbook and worksheets."

- "I will honor the range of reading abilities of my students by providing topical materials on a variety of reading levels" versus "I use the basal reader."

- "I will allow my students to take their learning as far as they want" versus "I keep everyone at the same place at the same time."

- "I will communicate with my students and parents electronically" versus "They can hope to catch me after class or at home in the evenings."

- "I will give parents real-time access to how their children are performing in my class" versus "I send out report cards and have two parent-teacher conferences a year."

- "I will use the information gathered from computerized value-added testing to know exactly what my individual students' strengths and weakness are" versus "I use whole-group instruction."

- "I will stay current on best educational practices using online databases, electronic mailing lists, professional blogs, and a myriad of news sources" versus "I can go to a conference once a year if my school pays for it and read shared professional journals if they get to me."

- "I will create a personal learning network with educational leaders, experts, and colleagues using e-mail and social networks" versus "I try to remember the advice of the instructor in my college methods class from 1980."

- "I will collaborate with my peers from around the world" versus "I stay behind my classroom door."

- "I will save time by drawing on the generosity and genius of others who have created and shared digital versions of lesson plans, handbooks, templates, guidelines, reading lists, and more" versus "I use the teacher's guide."

Survival tip: If we wish for students to master 21st-century skills, we need to model them.

CHAPTER SIX

Managing Disruptive Technologies in the Classroom

I don't have A.D.D. I'm just ignoring you.

—*Student T-shirt*

By its disruptive nature, technology has the potential to radically transform our current model of education, making today's school compared to tomorrow's educational experience look like the Victrola compared to the iPad. Technology may well be a meteor, and many teachers may be the unsuspecting dinosaurs. Scary stuff.

Might technology . . .

- Eliminate the need for bricks-and-mortar schools when classes can be conducted online?
- Eliminate the need for paper textbooks and study materials when all students have personal computing devices?
- Eliminate whole-group instruction when there is enough data on all students to personalize education for each learner?
- Eliminate lectures, tests, and core curricula as students use technology in a project-based learning environment?

Yet many classroom teachers are less concerned about the disruptive technologies of an indefinite future than they are about the "distractive" technologies that are here today.

Their ability to distract has put the use of student-owned laptops, netbooks, cell phones, handheld devices, iPods and MP3 players, and portable game players on the banned list in many classrooms. Educators are discovering that students are more interested in online resources like social networking sites, game sites, chat, and streaming media than they are in classroom lectures or textbook chapters about the Crimean War, square roots, or past participles.

"Those darned kids are just listening to the filthy lyrics of rap music on their iPods instead of my lecture," pretty much summarizes the argument. No device, no access, no distraction, many teachers reason.

As I have learned from my experiences both as an instructor and as a student, technology can indeed be a distraction in any learning environment. I find it discouraging to say the least when a participant in one of my "enthralling" workshops starts texting or banging out something on the keyboard instead of hanging on to each brilliant nugget of wisdom emanating from the front of the room.

But then again, I've found reading my e-mail more interesting than more than a few lectures myself.

How do we, as teachers, compete with Facebook, tablets, cell phones, netbooks, and text messaging? How do we manage the distractive qualities of technology in our classroom? Moreover, how do we use these very technologies to actually improve teaching and learning?

Let me say up front that there is no one-size-fits-all set of practices for managing or using student technologies. Different sources of technology (classroom mini-labs, one-to-one laptop projects, laptop carts, or student-owned technologies) will result in different amounts of access, various levels of uniformity of applications and functionality, and uncertain connections to online resources. Different teaching styles, different age levels, and different learning outcomes will make some technology uses practical and others not.

Nor is there a simple, easy solution to students' "tuning out." Some of us were distracted by doodling, the view from classroom windows, and especially cute classmates even before there were computers.

 Survival tip: Good teachers have never relied on a single method, a single approach, or a single tool to teach; and good teachers will not always use a single technology in a single way. As an effective teacher, you can use the technology available to you in ways that make sense to you.

Some Approaches to Managing Technology in the Classroom

Here are some common approaches teachers take to manage technology in their classroom:

1. **Ban it.** This has been the first and most common approach to dealing with distractive technologies—especially student-owned devices. Simply create a policy or rule for the classroom that forbids their use. And ignore any school-provided student technologies available to you.

   Keeping technologies out of classrooms is a temporary strategy that is unsustainable in the long run. Information devices are getting smaller, more affordable, and more powerful. They are increasingly an extension of everyone's brains—both adults and children. There is a growing movement to unblock an increasing number of Web sites in districts in which educators and students have learned the positive value of these resources.

   Where such devices are banned, student use often simply goes underground, with students texting from within pockets, hiding earbuds under hair and hoods, or simply concealing devices behind books or in desks.

   Parents see cell phones as tools for helping keep their children safe, insisting their children carry them in case of an emergency. Parents who have purchased laptops and tablets and smartphones want their children to be able to take educational advantage of these devices.

   Because a growing number of educators, parents, and students see the educational value of such devices, a classroom-, school-, or districtwide ban simply won't work.

2. **Do business as usual, let distracted students be distracted, and let the chips fall where they may.** It's tempting to simply rationalize that we should just let students tune out in the classroom, let them focus in on their YouTube videos, and let the natural consequences of such actions happen. Yet ethically we have always had a professional obligation to make sure all students are engaged in our classrooms. Besides, it's hard on the ego when students who pay no attention in class do better on your tests and assignments than those who do.

3. **Limit the use of technologies.** Establishing clear expectations of when and how technology can be used in one's classroom should be a standard classroom management practice. Setting reasonable rules is a simple task.

Many teachers find that such rules and expectations are best developed at the very beginning of the school year in collaboration with the students themselves.

Survival tip: Your "technology use" rule might be as simple as this: "Student-owned technologies, such as cell phones and laptops, may be used in the classroom when there is not a whole-group activity, when their use does not distract other students, and when the district's acceptable use policy is followed."

Teachers are finding that allowing students to use their own technologies in class can actually help with classroom management issues. Elona Harjes, who writes the Teachers at Risk blog, shared the following in response to a blog post of mine: "I have been encouraging my students to listen to music in class when I'm not giving instructions or explaining something. I let them use whatever digital gadget they have. Students who are listening to music seem less distracted and stay more on task."

4. **Enhance traditional educational practices.** Probably one of the most distractive technologies prevalent in the classroom is the cell phone. Students use them, of course, to text message their friends. There is the fear that they misuse them to cheat on tests and take photos that invade the privacy of other students.

But these modern cell phones also can help students learn. They can use them to . . .

- Exchange ideas with members of collaborative learning groups
- Request information from experts and send out surveys
- Listen to podcasts and view recorded videos of lessons
- Take notes
- Write to-do lists, set alarms, and enter assignment due dates in the built-in calendar
- Use the camera to take photographs of examples of items being studied (geometric shapes, effective communication examples, weather phenomena)
- Use an educational application or game on the device

- Respond to in-class surveys by sending text messages without needing a dedicated student response system device

Similar lists can be made for portable gaming devices, netbooks, and tablets.

No technology, no device, is inherently educational or recreational. It's all in how that device is used. Savvy teachers will figure out how to change "distraction" to "focus"—and use students' personal technologies to improve learning.

A Proposal Banning Pencils

Ex abusu non arguitur in usum. (The abuse of a thing is no argument against its use.)

When it comes to "technology" use in schools, every responsible educator's first concerns should be student safety and educational suitability. I am suggesting that we ban one of the most potentially harmful technologies of all—the pencil. We must eliminate pencils from schools for the following reasons:

1. A student might use a pencil to poke out the eye of another student.
2. A student might write a dirty word or, worse yet, a threatening note to another student with a pencil.
3. Students use pencils to write cheat sheets for tests.
4. One student might have a mechanical pencil, making those with wooden ones feel bad.
5. The pencil might get stolen.
6. Pencils break and need repairing all the time.
7. Kids who have pencils might doodle instead of working on their assignments or listening to the teacher.

Oh, sure, kids *might* actually use a pencil to take notes or compose a paper—but really, what's the chance of that?

Sounds pretty absurd, doesn't it? But listen to the reasons teachers and administrators give for banning iPods and MP3 players from the classroom:

1. They might get stolen.
2. They make kids who can't afford them feel bad.

3. Kids might listen to them instead of to the teacher.
4. Who knows what kinds of lyrics the kids might be listening to?
5. Kids might listen to test answers.

Oh, sure, kids *might* actually use them to study; to replay their French vocabulary lesson; or to listen to audiobooks, an NPR program, or a teacher-created podcast lecture—but really, what's the chance of that?

I cringe whenever I hear of a district or school "banning" cell phones, student blogs, e-mail, flash drives, chat, personally owned laptops, or game sites, remembering when student access to the Internet itself was hotly debated in the mid-1990s. Each of these technologies can and does have positive educational uses. Each of these technologies is a big part of many kids' lives outside of school. And yes, each of these technologies has the *potential* for misuse.

One of my biggest worries has always been that by denying access in school to technologies that students find useful and meaningful, we make school more and more irrelevant to our "Net Gen" students.

My experience is that the more familiar educators are with a new technology, the less likely they are to restrict its use by students. When we old-timers experience a technology's benefit ourselves, we better understand its benefit to students.

Using Technology in the Classroom to Support Student Learning

One very simple way to start thinking about how individual classroom technologies can stop being distracting and start being engaging is to begin with common classroom practices and add a technology "upgrade" as suggested in Chapter Four. Nearly any common teaching strategy or practice can be enhanced by the judicious use of technology. For example:

Lectures can be supplemented by polling students with a cell phone response system. Other teachers record their lessons, post them to a video streaming and downloading site, and allow students to view them multiple times on their phones or laptops. Some teachers allow students to record their lectures and instructions for later review with MP3 players.

Worksheets and study guides that may previously have been distributed as paper can be moved to electronic forms, using tools like Google Docs, or downloaded in a desktop word processing template format using a file-sharing site. Completed work can be saved and shared online or moved to a teacher's drop box, cutting down on printing costs and reducing the paper chase.

Learning games in physical form have long been an educational mainstay (spelldown, anyone?). Educational games accessible via mobile devices run the gamut from "flash card" reviews to sophisticated online worlds. **Manipulatives** have made a successful transition from cardboard and wood to digital formats, especially on touch screen devices, as demonstrated by Montessori's iPad and iPhone math applications. (See the section Computer Games in the Classroom later in this chapter.)

Assigned textbook readings can be supplemented or supplanted by more lively writings accessed online. E-books, both free and commercial, are available in the universal EPUB and PDF formats and can be read on a wide range of devices.

Written expository papers are no longer the only format through which students can share their understanding of a subject. Videos, audio recordings, and multimedia presentations allow students to display multiple talents, are more likely to ask for creativity, and are less subject to plagiarism.

The key to the value of any of these "technology-enhanced" activities is that there is *a genuine benefit* gained by adding a technology component. A criticism may be that this type of use is simply maintaining the traditional model of education. If traditional assignments and activities are going to be used by teachers, they should be made as engaging and interactive as possible.

> **Survival tip:** Asking students to use technology productively does not eliminate the need for a teacher's visual monitoring of student activities. The best way to reduce misuse of technology may still be the occasional walk among student desks.

You can use technology to teach **21st-century skills.** The increased amounts and kinds of technologies available to students in the classroom may spur schools to make the necessary changes to prepare students for academic, career, and civic success in the future.

Information problem solving is enabled by students' ability to access information sources from within the classroom. Individual students can be designated as "Google jockeys" to research questions that come up during class discussions.

Whereas younger students may be given small "everyday" problems to research, older students may work independently or in groups on genuine problems and questions related to a subject. One possible classroom structure would be to allocate a small percentage of class time to set out a problem or problems, a large percentage to do research on the problems, and the remainder of the class to report and discuss findings.

Students' ability to do inquiry using primary sources can be facilitated by student devices. Taking polls, conducting and recording interviews, and taking photographs are all good uses of those "problematic" cell phones.

The electronic provision of materials allows for true **differentiated instruction,** even **individualization.** Using the results of formative tests, teachers can give students access to learning materials to meet specific learning styles (visual, auditory, verbal) and to meet specific learning needs (for example, different reading levels). Students needing remediation in a math concept, for example, can complete an online tutorial and practice during class. Students with special needs have long had their particular requirements met through adaptive and adoptive technologies. The question we might ask is, What if all children can be considered as having "special needs"?

Accessing **collaborative online workspaces** is possible when enough students can get to wikis, blogs, and online productivity tools that allow for sharing and joint creation of work. Collaborative work helps keep kids on task because there is a certain degree of peer pressure brought to bear on slackers. Collaborative activities do not require that a one-to-one device-to-student ratio be in place—one laptop per team is often better than one per student.

Online collaborative tools enable the "conversation" to continue past class time—at home, in study halls, anywhere students have access to an Internet connection. Such communication vehicles have been shown to "bring out" the comments of shy students. And publication for an audience of peers raises many students' level of concern about the quality of their work.

Interaction with students from other countries and cultures is possible with communication technologies like VoIP (Voice over Internet Protocol) programs, chat, and e-mail. "Keypals" have long been a staple of creating global communities of learners, with students sharing observations and perspectives on issues from different cultural standpoints. The Flat Classroom® Project is a popular and powerful effort to expand this connectivity using a variety of classroom technology tools.

Personal communication and computing devices are here to stay—in society in general and in our classrooms. An increasing number of educators are writing about and sharing practical strategies for using technology productively in the classroom. Seek out those specific projects and applications and turn those supposedly distractive technologies into technologies that make your classroom more effective.

These Horses Are Already Out of the Barn

All truth passes through three stages. First, it is ridiculed. Second, it is violently opposed. Third, it is accepted as being self-evident.

—*Arthur Schopenhauer*

There are some educational realities we can't change, even if we wanted to. These educational technology resources, annoyances, and conditions are here to stay despite some educators' denial, resistance, and fast grip on the status quo. The sooner teachers accept that these things are a permanent part of the educational landscape, the sooner attention will be paid to using them positively and productively.

Here is my short list of things that are just *not* going to go away (although the names may change):

- Cell phones in schools
- Student-owned netbooks, laptops, and PDAs in schools
- Deficiencies in Internet filters and filter work-arounds for school-filtered Internet sites
- Web 2.0 tools—wikis, blogs, Ning, Flickr, Facebook
- Wikipedia
- Google Search
- Online term papers available for download
- YouTube
- Tasteless Web sites loved by middle school students
- Computer games
- Expectation of Wi-Fi access by students, staff, and visitors
- E-books and e-textbooks
- Music downloading and file sharing
- Texting and the shorthand used by students when texting (OMG!)
- Computerized testing
- Online classes and online schools

Computer Games in the Classroom

The debate rages in many schools on the role of computer and online games in education. Do you use games in—or ban games and gamers from—your classroom?

Ten Reasons for Games

1. Games keep kids busy who might otherwise be disturbing other kids.
2. Playing games gives teeth to the threat, "If you don't follow the rules you will lose your computer privileges."
3. Games give kids practice with social skills when they work in teams.
4. Games give kids practice learning about strategy, logic, and problem solving.
5. Games teach content.
6. Games build reading and math skills.
7. Games build research skills when students are looking for information about game strategies or solutions to puzzles.
8. Games build intergenerational conversations and relationships. (Four out of ten American *adults* turn to video games as their primary source of entertainment.)
9. Games get kids into libraries who might not otherwise go there, increasing the likelihood of books' being checked out.
10. Games build a positive association with school that might not otherwise be there for a lot of kids.

Three Reasons for Banning Games

1. Kids playing games might be using resources (computers, bandwidth, chairs, oxygen) that other kids might need to do "real" schoolwork.
2. Kids playing games find school fun, and we all know life isn't about fun.
3. Playing games is against school rules.

Let's be clear that there are games and there are games—just like there are movies and there are movies, and there are books and there are books. Games vary widely in type, from first-person shoot-'em-ups to skill attainment tutors with complex management programs. They vary in taste, rating, maturity level, and even factual accuracy.

The question shouldn't be Do we permit students to play games? but rather What games should we allow our students to play?

What criteria might a teacher use when selecting games for the classroom?

- Age appropriateness
- Content that is aligned to the curriculum

- Minimal technical requirements

- Low cost

- Such features as being able to turn off the sound, to save, and to create individual accounts

- Home accessibility

- Users' ability to create their own environments, levels, and missions and exhibit creativity and problem-solving skills

A checklist not unlike that used to select other educational media can and should be used when selecting games.

However, another standard might also be considered that goes beyond a simple checklist. Author-educator Marc Prensky (2005) differentiates between complex and simple games, arguing that most adults have a negative opinion of games because they associate the term *game* with the games of their childhood—card and board games, recreational pursuits meant to pass rainy afternoons. Prensky surmises, "Because of these formative game-playing experiences growing up, when today's teacher (or parent or educator) hears the word game, their first reaction is: 'trivial.' And they don't want this 'trivial' stuff to be part of their child's ... 'serious' education. So they reject games out of hand as a serious learning tool" (p. 3).

Instead, Prensky argues, we should be thinking about "complex" games, those that take ten to one hundred hours to complete. These games require "a player to learn a wide variety of often new and difficult skills and strategies, and to master these skills and strategies by advancing through dozens of ever-harder 'levels.' Doing this often requires both outside research and collaboration with others while playing" (p. 7).

Current complex game titles include *SimCity, Civilization III, Rise of Nations, Age of Empires, Age of Kings, Harry Potter, Lord of the Rings, Myst, Riven, EverQuest, City of Heroes, World of Warcraft,* all the *Tycoon* games, *John Madden Football, Medal of Honor, Full Spectrum Warrior,* and *America's Army.*

Consider adding games as a resource in your classroom. They're not just motivational, they're good for kids.

Why You Should Let Your Students Use the Internet for Nonacademic Purposes

Kids should be allowed to use the Internet at school for nonacademic purposes. Period.

Pursuing personal and recreational interests (so long as they're not illegal) should actually be encouraged, especially in our classrooms. Why? Personal Internet use . . .

1. **Gives teeth to the threat of suspending Internet use for disciplinary reasons.** If Johnny likes accessing the world soccer scores each morning on the classroom computers, he may think twice about doing something that will suspend his Internet "privileges." If students are only allowed "academic" use of the Internet, how many will actually find such a consequence punitive?

2. **Gives practice in reading, researching, problem solving, and being creative.** Kids using the Internet are practicing a lot of skills. If fluency, vocabulary building, and intrinsic motivation for reading are goals, what difference does it make whether a student is reading the reading primer or a Web site of personal interest?

3. **Shows consistency with other formats.** Does your library carry *Sports Illustrated* and *Seventeen*? Have you developed a classroom fiction collection for voluntary free reading? Do you have board games in your classroom? So why treat digital resources differently than you do paper ones?

4. **Creates a positive school atmosphere.** We have got to get over the idea that schooling has to be serious and boring to be effective. Think how much easier our work would be if kids actually wanted to be in school.

5. **Helps close the digital divide.** Many students still do not have access to online resources from home. It seems somehow cruel and unusual to deny this huge cultural influence to some students.

A common reason for disallowing "recreational" computer use has been that computers and network bandwidth may be in short supply. The reasoning goes that schoolwork (writing papers, doing academic research, and so on) takes precedence over "fun." For all the reasons mentioned in this chapter, we need to rethink this blanket policy and find other means of fairly allocating computer time.

Commonsense Practices for Safe and Ethical Technology Use

*I*t wasn't a week after our district had given e-mail addresses to about six hundred middle school students when a teacher stormed up to me, upset and confused. "They're sending each other e-mail with bad language! What are we going to do?"

"What would you do if your students were passing paper notes to each other with bad language?" I asked.

The teacher's face lit up. She was back on familiar ground. "We have harassment policies to handle that."

This teacher was one of the most knowledgeable, competent educators with whom I'd ever worked. Her classroom had been wired, and the kids had had access to the Internet and other technological goodies longer than anyone else in the school. Through a long career of working with middle school students and parents, she had dealt successfully with a huge range of behaviors and situations.

Yet like many adults working in schools, the teacher did not always feel comfortable making decisions about the proper use of technology, especially networked technologies. Adding to the tension are stories in the media of young people "sexting," hacking into computer files, viewing online pornography, and placing themselves at risk by corresponding with strangers online. Digital resources also add a layer of complexity to the chronic issues of plagiarism and copyright abuse that are already confusing for most educators.

Not knowing how to use a technology safely is frightening. And most rational people tend to avoid the things that scare them. Yet responsible teachers understand that knowing how to use information technologies both ethically and safely is a critical 21st-century skill for their students and for them.

Teacher's Day-to-Day Security Guide

Let's start with some practical advice for you, the teacher, as a technology user. Recommended security manuals for school districts are about two hundred pages long. Here are the most critical things you need to know and practice as a classroom teacher—in just a few pages. Please read carefully.

HARDWARE SECURITY

Computers and other hardware can be stolen and damaged through both carelessness and maliciousness.

- Computers should be on a firm surface, well away from desk and table edges to prevent them from being accidentally pushed off.
- Computer cords and cables should be in molding, raceways, or cable trays to prevent damage both to the computers and to anyone who might trip over them.
- If your computer is a laptop, use a security cable to lock it to your desk if it is left unattended.
- All hardware needs to be purchased through the district so it can be inventoried and engraved with a school ID. You will also have the assurance that the equipment will be compatible with software and computer systems your school uses.
- If you use your school computer at home or take it to meetings or conferences, be sure your homeowner's insurance covers it if it's lost or damaged. Take special precautions at airport security checks, at hotels, and in meetings to make sure your computer is not left unattended. Most hotels will provide an in-room safe or a secure area at the reception desk where you can safely store a laptop computer when you are not in your room.

Survival tip: Invest in an inexpensive computer cable that secures your laptop to a desk, table, or other permanent fixture. Small teeth fit in a slot in the side of your computer that can be opened and closed using a combination lock or key. Such a lock is a deterrent, not a guarantee, however.

- Under no circumstances should you open (or attempt to open) your computer's case. You may damage the computer, and you run the risk of getting a severe electric shock. Let a technician handle any repairs that require the case to be opened.

- Unless you need them on your hard drive, keep files that have confidential data at school on a file server or in the cloud. That way, if your computer does get lost or stolen, private data won't get in the wrong hands.

Digital records, communications, and intellectual property are as valuable and important as physical property, despite their intangible nature. An increasing amount of important and confidential data is transmitted and stored electronically in schools. Safeguards to protect these data are essential, and using them is a professional obligation.

PASSWORDS

As a teacher, you are responsible for a variety of passwords, including those for the student information system, your e-mail accounts, individual education plans, progress reports, grade book programs, your screen saver, and your voice mail. All passwords . . .

- Should be unique for each application
- Should be changed on a regular, frequent basis
- Should be composed of both letters and numbers for highest security
- Should be composed of a string of characters not found in a dictionary
- Should be kept in a secure place if written down
- Should never be given to anyone else, especially students
- Should never be given to a tech support person who is unknown to you

Survival tip: Creating a simple mnemonic that will help you meet the password requirements given here will save your sanity and keep you secure. For example, create a password using the current month number, your father's first name, and the initials of the program for which the password applies (for example, "04paulgb" for your grade book). Oh, and change your passwords each month.

Another View of Password Security

I've always had a suspicion that the requirement for a "strong" password really creates more security problems than it solves under most circumstances. Strong passwords require a minimum of twelve to fourteen characters, need to be a combination of numbers and upper- and lower-case letters, and are often required to be changed on a regular basis.

Such complexity leads normal people to write passwords down and hide them in a convenient place—in the top desk drawer, under the desk calendar, or on a sticky note adhering to the monitor.

The rationale for strong passwords is that they are harder to discover if one runs a fancy password-guessing program to crack a computer security system. Such programs rapidly try all common words and names in an attempt to gain access.

So the question I have to ask is: Which is more likely, that a middle school student will have access to a cracking program or that he or she will know that passwords can be found under the teacher's desk blotter?

There are compromises that involve mnemonic clues for remembering stronger passwords:

- Adding a date to a child's or pet's name ("sammy411")
- Substituting numbers or symbols for letters ("r0o$evelt")
- Creating an acronym ("1itln"—one is the loneliest number)
- Writing the password down but with a change in a single character that one can actually remember

None of these are recommended by computer security experts, I am sure. Be thankful I don't work for the CIA.

And although passwords are important, remember that social hacking—directly taking advantage of a person's trusting nature—remains the number-one computer security threat. If you call people and say you are from so-and-so security firm and are conducting an audit and need to verify their password, a high percentage of people happily divulge that information.

 Survival tip: Treat passwords with the same care you would a paper grade book, the key to your classroom, or the code of your ATM card.

BACKUPS

It is *your* responsibility to maintain at least one backup copy of your self-created school documents (word-processed files, presentations, and so on). You should also regularly create backup copies of your grade book data, stored e-mail messages, e-mail address book, calendar, and to-do list if this information is stored on your hard drive rather than online. Back up all files on at least a monthly basis, and more often if you are working on a critical project. You need to ask yourself, *What would I lose if my computer's hard drive were to die right now?*

Your district may provide online file space for you to do this. You may also choose to use writeable CD-ROMs or DVDs to create copies of your files if your computer is so equipped. These backup disks should be kept in a secure place outside your school building. An inexpensive external hard drive may be the most convenient option.

The district is responsible for creating backups of data from districtwide applications like the student information system, but you must create backups of your own files.

Where Is My Data the Safest?

I don't know about you, but I like to keep a few hundred thousand dollars' worth of gold bullion around just in case of natural disaster.*

The question is—Where to keep it? I have a number of options:

1. I can keep it nice and close where I can keep my eye on it—under my bed.
2. I can buy a home safe and keep it locked.
3. I can rent a safe deposit box and keep it in a bank.

The first two of these options certainly offer some psychological comfort. Knowing that those Krugerrands are close—where I can touch them, see them, and protect them—on the surface might seem like the safest course of action. After all, I have the biggest stake in keeping my stash secure.

But on reflection, most of us quickly realize that our valuables are safest in the bank. The bank employs professional security staff. Its safe is a lot bigger and stronger than what we can afford. And banks offer some degree of insurance against loss.

Yes, banks are sometimes robbed, and one could get mugged carrying one's loot to or from the bank, but the odds of those things happening are minuscule compared to the probability of having one's home burgled. Electronic fund transfers and using a bill-pay service are safer and more reliable than writing a paper check.

So if it makes sense to keep one's physical valuables in a bank, why does it not also make sense to keep one's data (like e-mail) on an application service provider? These off-site services (like Gmail) hire professional staff, give strong security to users, and maintain 99.9 percent uptime rates. It's like keeping your data in a bank instead of under your mattress (or on your computer).

*I'm just kidding. Please don't burgle my house. Or if you do, take the cat.

VIRUSES

Computer viruses and other malware are small pieces of computer code that may have the ability to destroy data on your computer or on computer networks. Needless to say, technology departments take extreme precautions to protect their computer users from these programs, which are spread as e-mail attachments, hidden in programs downloaded from Internet Web sites, and embedded as macros in word-processed and other documents. Although the firewall (a computerized filter that screens all data coming into the district) and the spam filter catch many viruses, new viruses are constantly being created, and no filter is perfect.

As a teacher, you can minimize your exposure to viruses if you . . .

- Never open an attachment you were not expecting, even from someone known to you. (E-mail addresses can be spoofed—used by someone to whom they do not belong.)
- Never download programs from unknown sources on the Internet (or let your children download them).
- Turn the "macro" feature off or turn on "macro security" in word processing and spreadsheet programs.
- Scan your computer regularly using a virus protection program, especially if you have a laptop or desktop computer you use both at home and at school.

DATA PRIVACY

Protecting our students' privacy is a professional responsibility. This means knowing the laws, district policies, and building guidelines about what student information can be shared and with whom. Increasingly this also means indirectly protecting student records and personal information by following the password guidelines listed earlier in this chapter.

Survival tip: Use a screen saver that automatically starts after a short period of inactivity on the computer in your classroom so that screen contents are not easily viewed when you are away from your desk. For added security, a password to exit the screen saver should be set.

Parental permission forms need to be completed prior to posting photographs or student work on the school Web site. Students' last names, e-mail addresses, or other identifying information should not appear on the school Web site. Readers wishing to comment on student work that may appear on the school Web site should be writing to the teacher's e-mail account.

Students need to recognize that school-provided e-mail accounts, file storage space, and log-ins and usage logs may be viewed by school authorities and law enforcement officers if necessary. Your district's Internet acceptable use policy probably has a statement similar to this one: "Users should expect only limited privacy in the contents of personal files on the school district system." Most districts only exercise the right to view student files when there has been suspicion of wrongdoing rather than employing a continuously running monitoring program.

> **Survival tip:** If you read no other school board policy, read your school's Internet acceptable use policy. Some explicit statements may prohibit users from using school district Internet resources or accounts to do the following:
>
> 1. Access, upload, download, or distribute pornographic, obscene, or sexually explicit material
> 2. Transmit or receive obscene, abusive, or sexually explicit language
> 3. Violate any local, state, or federal statute
> 4. Vandalize, damage, or disable the property of another person or organization
> 5. Access another person's materials, information, or files without the implied or direct permission of that person
> 6. Violate copyright laws, or otherwise use another person's property without the person's prior approval or proper citation, including by downloading or exchanging pirated software or by copying software to or from any school computer
> 7. Use the Internet for unauthorized commercial or financial gain

PERSONAL PRIVACY

As e-mail and Internet users, teachers also need to follow guidelines to protect their own personal data and privacy. As a district employee, you are subject to the same acceptable use policy as your students, including the "limited privacy" rule just mentioned. Most districts use the "only as needed" approach to viewing staff e-mail and files.

If you use the Internet to purchase goods, sign up for newsletters, or complete surveys, you will be asked to provide personal information. Do so at your own risk. Some guidelines:

- Never give your social security number over the Internet. Be very careful to whom you supply your telephone number, e-mail address, mailing address, and other personal information.
- When making a purchase using a credit card on the Internet, make sure the site is reputable and "secure." A secure site's address will begin with "https" rather than simply "http."
- Limit the "cookies" your Internet browser will accept.
- Maintain two e-mail addresses: one that is used only for business or with those people you know, and one for commercial transactions, surveys, and so on. The second e-mail address can be a free account from a provider, such as Yahoo!, and can be easily changed if too much spam is being sent to your account.
- Regularly run a spyware detection program to find and eliminate hidden programs on your computer.

Helping Students Stay Ethical and Safe Online

Even very young children can quickly identify whether the behaviors in these examples are right or wrong:

- A boy finds a magazine with sexually explicit photographs and brings it to school. He shows its contents to others in his class, who become upset.
- A student steals a set of keys and uses them to gain access to the school office, where she changes her grades and views the grades of other students.
- A student reads a story in a library book, recopies it in his own writing, and submits it to the teacher as his own work.
- A student steals a book from a local store. She says the only reason she stole it was that she did not have the money to purchase it.

When students use technology, especially information technologies that consist of computers and computer networks, they are operating in a different world: a virtual world in which behaviors may not be as easily judged to be right or wrong. What would your students' responses be when given these situations?

- A girl downloads a sexually explicit picture from a site on the Internet on a computer in the school library. Her classmates can easily view the computer screen.

- A student finds the teacher's password to the information system and uses it to change his grade and view the grades of other students.

- A student uses the "copy" and "paste" commands to insert large parts of an electronic encyclopedia article into an assigned paper. She turns the paper in as her own work.

- A student makes a copy of a software program borrowed from another student to use on his computer at home.

Survival tip: A good way to analyze a technology ethics situation is by trying to find an analogy from the precomputer world.

WHAT'S DIFFERENT ABOUT TECHNOLOGY ETHICS?

Technology ethics have to do with the proper use of a wide range of telecommunication and data storage devices. Ethics is the branch of philosophy that deals with moral judgments, issues of right and wrong, and determining what behaviors are humane or inhumane. A simple way of defining an "ethical action" is that such an action does not have a damaging impact on oneself, other individuals, or society.

Safety is the flip side of the ethics coin. Online safety means learning how to protect oneself from the unethical behavior of others.

In direct or indirect ways, children begin to learn ethical values from birth. And although the family is assigned the primary responsibility for a child's ethical education, many of the ethical issues that surround technology pertain to societal and school behaviors and are an appropriate and necessary part of the school curriculum.

Why do technology ethics deserve special attention? There are a variety of reasons. Using technology to communicate and operate in a "virtual world," one that only exists within computers and computer networks, is a relatively new phenomenon that is not always well understood by many adults who received their primary education prior to computers' existence. Both fear and romance usually accompany new technologies, and both over- and underreactions to misuse are common. Popular media often make questionably ethical actions, such as breaking into secure computer systems, seem heroic.

One of the most significant reasons why computer ethics deserve special attention relates to our rather human ability to view one's actions in the intangible, virtual world of information technologies as being less serious than one's actions in the real world. Most of us, adults or children, would never contemplate walking into a store and shoplifting a physical computer program or music CD. Yet software and music piracy costs businesses billions of dollars each year. Most of us would never pick a lock, but guessing passwords to gain access to unauthorized information is a common activity. We may often say something online that we would never say in a face-to-face conversation.

Information technology misuse is often viewed, especially by the young, as a low-risk, gamelike challenge. Electronic fingerprints, footsteps, and other evidence of digital impropriety have historically been less detectable than physical evidence. There is a physical risk when breaking into a real office that does not exist when hacking into a computer database from home. Illegally copying a book is costly and time consuming; illegally copying an e-book can be done in seconds at no cost. The pornography viewed on a Web site seems to disappear as soon as the browser window is closed.

As the use of information technology spreads throughout society, and as its importance to our national economies and individual careers grows, everyone will need to make good ethical decisions when using computers.

BASICS OF TECHNOLOGY ETHICS: PRIVACY, PROPERTY, APPROPRIATE USE

Written guidelines for technology use should be made available to staff and students. These can be either adapted or original. Even if an entire school or district uses a single set of guidelines, each classroom teacher still needs to understand, teach, and model them.

Simple, easily remembered guidelines rather than long lists of specific rules are the best. Here are mine:

Johnson's Three Rules of Technology Ethics

1. **Privacy**—I will protect my privacy and respect the privacy of others.
2. **Property**—I will protect my property and respect the property of others.
3. **Appropriate use**—I will use technology in constructive ways and in ways that do not break the rules of my family, faith, school, or government.

Here are some common cases in which younger children will need to make ethical choices or will have the unethical actions of others affect them, categorized under the major headings of privacy, property, and appropriate use. These cases and others like them can be used to foster classroom discussion.

Privacy

Does my use of the technology violate the privacy of others, or am I giving information to others that I should not?

> John fills out a survey form on a computer game Web page. In the following weeks he receives several advertisements in the mail as well as dozens of e-mail messages about new computer games.

Children need to understand that businesses and organizations use information to market products. Personal information given to one organization may well be sold to others. An interesting discussion can revolve around how much a person would like a company to know about him or her. (Will a company that knows a lot about me use this information to customize products for me or only to manipulate me?)

> Adele "meets" Frank, who shares her interest in figure skating, in a chat room. After several conversations in the following weeks, Frank asks Adele for her home telephone number and address.

All individuals need to know that a stranger is a stranger, whether on the playground or on the Internet. The same rules we teach children about physical strangers apply to virtual strangers as well.

> The principal suspects Paul of using his school e-mail account to send offensive messages to other students. He asks the network manager to give him copies of Paul's e-mail.

Schools (and businesses) have the right to search student and employee files that are created and stored on school-owned computer hardware. Ask students if they know the school's search policy on lockers and book bags, and whether the same policy should be extended to computer storage devices.

Property

Do my actions respect the property of others, and am I taking the correct steps to keep my property safe?

> Jerry borrows Ben's game disks for *Monster Truck Rally II* and installs them on his home computer.

Students need to know that copyright law protects computer software. It is unlawful, as well as unethical, to make copies of computer programs without permission from or payment of the producer of those programs. It also needs to be understood that when purchasing software, one is usually only purchasing the right to use the software. The ownership of the code that makes up the program stays with the producer. This means that one cannot alter the program or resell copies of the program. The vast majority of software licenses require that one copy of a program be purchased for each computer on which it is to be run. The inability to pay for software is not a justification for illegal copying any more than the inability to pay for a book is any justification for shoplifting it from a bookstore.

> Cindy finds some good information about plant growth nutrients for her science fair project on Wikipedia. She uses the copy function of

the computer to take an entire paragraph from the article and paste it directly into her report. When she writes her report, she does not cite the source in her bibliography.

Plagiarism is easier than ever, thanks to the computer. Students need to understand when and how to cite sources in both print and electronic formats.

Fahad is upset with his friend George. He finds the flash drive on which George has been storing his essays and erases it.

Does deleting a file constitute the destruction of property? The magnetic medium of the drive and the plastic case are left intact. All that has changed is the polarization of some magnetic particles. Students need to learn to treat intellectual property, existing only in virtual spaces, the same way they would treat physical property and that the theft or destruction of such property is unethical (and unlawful).

Appropriate Use

Does this use of the technology have educational value, and is it in keeping with the rules of my family, my school, and my government?

Jack's class has been using a digital camera to take pictures for the school yearbook. Jack has found that he can use a computer program to change the photographs. He has used the program so far to make himself look like the tallest boy in the class, to blacken out the front tooth of a girl he doesn't like, and to give his teacher crossed eyes.

Although this example may seem frivolous or even like "good fun," journalistic integrity is a serious issue of which even young writers and photographers need to be aware. Deliberate distortion of events, whether through modifying words or through doctoring pictures, may harm those involved in the event as well as the reputation of the reporter.

Just for fun, thirteen-year-old Alice tells the other people on her electronic mailing list that she is twenty years old and a nursing student. Others on the list have begun e-mailing her health-related questions.

Disguising oneself, impersonating someone else, and other forms of "trying on" new personalities are common childhood and adolescent behaviors. The anonymity of the Internet limits such impersonation only to the degree that a student's lack of writing skills or sophistication of thought allows discovery. Role playing in a physical context is often seen as both healthy and educational. We need to help students ask when such activities are productive and when they might be harmful.

> Penelope has found a Web site that has "gross jokes" on it. She prints out the pages and shares them with her friends.

A good deal of Internet content, if not obscene, is certainly tasteless, offensive, and lacking in educational value. Schools should define—and teachers should help students understand—the qualities and conditions under which an item becomes inappropriate for school use. Students need to understand the concepts of pornography, racism, and sexism. Students may be exposed to information produced by hate groups and political extremists. Such experiences may be springboards to meaningful discussions about propaganda and issues of free speech.

STAYING SAFE ON THE READ-WRITE WEB

> Lonely when her parents are at work, Sarah spends a lot of time in chat rooms. One evening she meets a man who seems to "understand" her. After several weeks of communication, Sarah agrees to meet him in person.

> Miguel is devastated by a Web site that personally denigrates him that has been created by an unidentified bully.

> Linda is removed from the varsity volleyball team after she puts a picture of herself drinking at a party on her Facebook profile.

These incidents, modeled after actual events, cause teachers to worry anew about the safety of children and young adults using the Internet. The World Wide Web has rapidly changed from a read-only resource to one in which user input is not just allowed but encouraged. The development of online tools that allow content to be entered, uploaded, edited, displayed, and made public without having any programming skills has made this Web 2.0 possible.

And teachers are struggling to determine just how to deal with Problems 2.0.

WHAT ARE THE READ-WRITE WEB SAFETY CONCERNS, AND HOW VALID ARE THEY?

The social Web is creating a new set of concerns about students' safe and ethical behaviors on the Internet—behaviors less easily controlled by mechanical solutions, such as filters. These concerns include the following:

- **Stranger danger: protecting children from predators.** Pedophiles using the information gleaned from sites like Facebook are arguably the area of greatest concern to parents and educators. According to the National Center for Missing & Exploited Children, approximately one in seven youths (ten to seventeen years old) experiences a sexual solicitation or approach while online, and the Center warns parents about the possibility of physical abduction of their children ("Statistics," 2011). Other authorities doubt such figures, writing that in 2005 there were only one hundred known cases of child exploitation related to social networking sites nationwide and that most "sexual solicitation" is done among peers, not pedophiles. Studies also show that students at the greatest risk of online predation are those who are at the greatest risk in the physical world—children lacking good parental support (Magid and Collier, 2007).

- **Cyberbullying: protecting children from each other.** Cyberbullying can be defined as "sending or posting harmful, embarrassing, malicious, or cruel text or images using digital forms of communication." There are documented instances in which such activities have resulted in severe psychological damage to the victim. Cyberbullying incidents are growing.

- **TMI (Too Much Information): protecting children from themselves.** Children and young adults are most likely to do harm to themselves on the social Web by posting pictures and messages that portray them in a negative light. This information is then found and viewed by teachers, coaches, relatives, college admissions officers, and potential employers. Students don't understand that material once placed on the Internet and made public has the potential of *always* being accessible.

To put it simply, the danger to kids in the Web 2.0 comes not so much from what they may find online as from what they themselves may put online for others to find.

One knee-jerk reaction for keeping students "safe" in read-write environments has been to block *all* social networking resources—Facebook, blogs, wikis, YouTube, Flickr, and virtual worlds. What is problematic about a school district's decisions to block Web 2.0 tools is that these policies block by *format*, not *content*. In other words, because a student might place personal information on a blog, *all* blogs are blocked. This would be like a school banning all magazines because *Penthouse* is published in magazine format. Formats are content neutral, but many adults seem to be having a difficult time separating content from format.

Even if social networking sites are effectively blocked in schools, most students will still get access to them. Proxies and mobile networking devices allow the savvy student to avoid district filters.

Pioneering educators are finding exciting ways to make good use of Web 2.0 resources. Libraries are replacing their newsletters with blogs that can be rapidly updated and allow readers to respond. Teachers are using wikis to facilitate peer-reviewed and collaborative writing projects, including student-created textbooks. Social bookmarking sites are proving to be an efficient means of creating bibliographies and reading lists. Creative teachers are asking students to make Facebook-like profiles for literary characters. (Who *would* be on Juliet Capulet's list of friends?) Virtual worlds are allowing students to build historical places and reenact historical events. Schools are creating Facebook fan pages to inform a generation of parents and students who seem to be using social media rather than e-mail as their primary means of communication.

And the issues are larger than these resources simply being used to facilitate traditional learning experiences. As social networking becomes a primary means of political and cultural communication, students who do not have home Internet access will depend on school resources for full participation.

Obviously teachers must create a balance between the desire to pursue opportunities for engaging students and developing new teaching methods and the need to protect children. To think simple Internet filters will eliminate or even minimize the real risks associated with social networking is a dangerous misconception. It will take educating students about the appropriate use of the Web 2.0 to genuinely protect them.

WHAT STUDENTS NEED TO UNDERSTAND ABOUT TECHNOLOGY USE

It is quite obvious that students need to understand and apply both school rules and local and national laws that apply to information technology use. They need to know the consequences, both immediate and long-term, for society and themselves personally if they choose to act illegally or unethically.

Students also need to know that the ability of officials to catch individuals breaking these rules and codes of conduct is growing. Electronic fingerprints, virtual footprints, and broken digital locks are becoming more visible each day.

Students need to understand both their rights and their responsibilities related to information technology use. (In your school, is Internet access a right or a privilege?) As the Internet becomes a more indispensable source of information and learning activities, it may become viewed as an integral part of one's right to an education. We have an obligation to teach students that they have a right to due process if charged as being in violation of rules or laws. Our acceptable use policies need to articulate what that due process entails. On a practical level, students need to know how to protect themselves and their data from strangers, hackers, computer viruses, and unauthorized access.

Responsible teachers recognize that schools must give students the understandings and skills they need to stay safe—not just in school but also outside of school where most Internet use by young people occurs. Overfiltered school networks set up a false sense of security; the real world of the Internet is quite different from the Internet at school.

Teachers who address safe and ethical Internet use proactively . . .

1. **Articulate personal values when using technology.** Talk to students about ethical online conduct and set clear limits about what is allowed and what is not allowed. All staff members must be knowledgeable about the school's acceptable use policy and work to help their students understand it. A district's current acceptable use policy should include language about posting private information about oneself and others. Examine any bullying policies you might have to make sure they cover electronic bullying as well as physical bullying.

2. **Stress the consideration and application of principles rather than reliance on a detailed set of rules.** Although sometimes more difficult to enforce in a consistent manner, a set of a few guidelines rather than a lengthy compilation of specific rules is more beneficial to students in the long run. By applying guidelines rather than following rules, students engage in higher-level thinking processes and learn behaviors that will continue into their next classroom, their home, and their adult lives.

3. **Model ethical behaviors.** All of us learn more from what others *do* than from what they *say*. Verbalization of how we personally make decisions is a very powerful teaching tool, but it's useless to lecture about safe and appropriate use when we might not follow our own rules.

4. **Build student trust.** If an inappropriate site is accidentally accessed, use the incident to teach some strategies about using clues in search result findings to discriminate between relevant and nonrelevant sites. ("Jose, when the search results say 'hot chicks xxx,' that probably won't be a source for your report on chickens.")

5. **Encourage discussion of ethical issues.** "Cases," whether from news sources or from actual school events, can provide superb discussion starters and should be used when students are actually learning computer skills. Students need practice in creating meaningful analogies between the virtual world and the physical world. How is reading another person's e-mail without his or her permission like and unlike reading his or her physical mail?

6. **Accept the fact that students will make mistakes.** Coach John Wooden famously said, "If you're not making mistakes, then you're not doing anything." Learning is about making errors and figuring out how not to repeat them. When a middle school student shares her password with a friend who

then destroys her files, that is a recoverable mistake—one that she might remember before sharing personal data as an adult.

7. **Allow students personal use of the Internet.** If Internet-enabled computers are not being used for curricular purposes, let students research topics of personal interest (that are not inherently dangerous or pornographic). The best reason for allowing this is that students are far less likely to risk the loss of Internet privileges if that means losing access to sites they enjoy.

8. **Reinforce ethical behaviors and react to students' misuse of technology.** Technology-use behaviors—good or bad—need to be treated no differently than other behaviors, and the consequences of such behaviors should be equal. Try not to overreact to incidents of technological misuse. If a student were caught reading *Playboy* in paper form, it's doubtful we'd suspend all his reading privileges.

9. **Create environments that help students avoid temptations.** Computer screens that are easily monitored and the requirement that users must log into and out of network systems help remove the opportunities for technology misuse. Your presence is a far more effective means of ensuring good behavior than filtering software.

10. **Assess children's understanding of ethical concepts.** Do not give technology-use privileges until a student has demonstrated that he or she knows and can apply school policies. Test appropriate use prior to students' gaining online access.

Survival tip: Keep evidence on file that students have been tested on their understanding of Internet acceptable use in case there is a question of whether there has been instruction on appropriate use (for example, if a parent suggests, "Little Johnny didn't know any better").

11. **Educate their students and themselves.** Aware teachers are using online curricula from organizations like iLearn, ConnectSafely, and Responsible Netizen to inform themselves and their children. These ready-made curricula are simple to integrate when teaching Internet safety units.

Survival tip: Look for a safety curriculum that is balanced and practical rather than "fear based."

12. **Educate parents about ethical technology use.** Through school newsletters, talks at parent organization meetings, and school orientation programs, teachers can inform parents and enlist their aid in teaching and enforcing good technology practices.

Will doing these things guarantee that a student will never get in trouble or in danger online? Of course not. But schools never have been able to guarantee students' physical safety either. What schools must be able to demonstrate is that they have shown due diligence: that they have taken serious steps to prevent harm from occurring. This means that a formal, documented plan—one that includes the actions just listed—is necessary. Installing Internet filters alone does not constitute due diligence.

Ethical instruction needs to be ongoing. A single lesson, a single unit, or a single curriculum strand will not suffice. Teachers should integrate ethical instruction into every activity that uses technology.

Guidelines for Educators Using Social and Educational Networking Sites

Teachers have a professional image to uphold, and how we conduct ourselves online has an impact on this image. As reported by the media, there have been instances in which educators have demonstrated professional misconduct by engaging in inappropriate dialogue about their school, their students, or both or by posting pictures and videos of themselves engaged in inappropriate activity online. Some educators mistakenly feel that being online shields them from having their personal lives examined. But an educator's online identity is very public and can cause serious repercussions if his or her behavior is careless.

One of the hallmarks of online networks, both social and educational, is the ability to "friend" others—to create a group of individuals who share interests and personal news. Think twice before accepting invitations to friend students within personal social networking sites. When students gain access to your network of friends and acquaintances and are able to view personal photos and communication, the student-teacher dynamic is altered. By friending students, you may be providing more information than you should share in an educational setting. It is important to maintain a professional relationship with students to avoid anything that could cause bias in the classroom.

Student-teacher interaction on educational networking sites has value, however. Collaboration, resource sharing, and student-to-teacher and student-to-student dialogue can all be facilitated by the appropriate use of educational networking tools. Such interactivity is a critical component of any online class and can greatly enhance face-to-face classes. Yet because this is a new means of communication, some guidelines are in order for educational networking as well.

For the protection of your professional reputation, consider the following guidelines:

On Public Social Networking Sites, Such as Facebook . . .

- Do not accept students as friends on personal social networking sites. Decline any student-initiated friend requests.

- Do not initiate friendships with students.

- Remember that people classified as friends have the ability to download and share your information with others.

- Post only what you want the world to see. Imagine your students, their parents, and your administrator visiting your site. On a social networking site, once you post something it may be available even after you have removed it from your account—photos or comments may be shared widely in only minutes—and can never be recovered.

- Do not discuss students or coworkers or publicly criticize school policies or personnel.

- Visit your profile's security and privacy settings. At a minimum, educators should have all privacy settings set to "only friends." Making your information visible to "friends of friends" and "networks and friends" opens your content to a large group of unknown people. Your privacy and that of your family may be a risk.

> **Survival tip:** If you would like to use Facebook to communicate with your students and parents, set up a Facebook fan page for posting only school-related information.

On Educational Networking Sites . . .

- Let your administrator, fellow teachers, and parents know about your educational network.

- When they are available, use school-supported networking tools.

- Do not say or do anything you would not say or do as a teacher in the classroom. (Remember that all forms of online communication are stored and can be monitored.)

- Have a clear statement of purpose and outcomes for the use of the networking tool.

- Establish a code of conduct for all network participants.
- Do not post images that include students without parental release forms on file.
- Pay close attention to the site's security settings and allow only approved participants to access the site.

On *All* Networking Sites . . .

- Do not use commentary deemed to be defamatory, obscene, proprietary, or libelous. Exercise caution in regard to exaggeration, colorful language, guesswork, obscenity, copyrighted materials, legal conclusions, and derogatory remarks or characterizations.
- Weigh whether a particular post puts your effectiveness as a teacher at risk.
- Due to security risks, be cautious when installing the external applications that work with the social networking site. Examples of these applications are calendar programs and games.
- Run updated malware protection to avoid infections of spyware and adware that social networking sites might place on your computer.
- Be careful not to fall for phishing scams that arrive via e-mail or on your wall, providing a link for you to click that leads to a fake log-in page.
- If you learn of information through a social networking site that falls under the mandatory reporting guidelines, you must report it as required by law.

Please stay informed and cautious in the use of all new networking technologies.

Social Networking Scenarios

For each of the following situations,

1. Discuss the possible ethical issues of the situation
2. Determine if the safety or well-being of anyone is at stake
3. Consider what advice, strategy, or policy you would recommend to individuals or schools based on this scenario
4. Share any real-life incidents related to the scenario

SOCIAL NETWORKING SCENARIO 1: MR. BLAKE AND JENNIFER

High school social studies teacher Mr. Blake has been adding students as friends to his Facebook page, using the forum to answer questions and guide classroom-related discussions. Lately some students have begun asking personal questions about Mr. Blake's relationships and life choices. Jennifer's mother, who monitors Jennifer's Internet use, feels uncomfortable about this and brings it to the attention of the principal.

SOCIAL NETWORKING SCENARIO 2: MS. OLSON'S CAMPING TRIP

Sixth-grade teacher Ms. Olson posted pictures of the camping trip she and her husband took last summer in her public Flickr album. In one of the photos she is smoking what looks suspiciously like a marijuana cigarette. One of her students finds the photos and shows her friends.

SOCIAL NETWORKING SCENARIO 3: JUAN AND PHILIP TRADE INSULTS

HHH Middle School students are using Google Docs as a writing tool and as a means of doing peer reviewing. Juan and Philip have used the platform to exchange messages that involve name-calling and racial slurs. Philip's parents object when his account is suspended for two weeks, believing it will hurt his academic progress.

SOCIAL NETWORKING SCENARIO 4: THE SOCIAL NETWORKING BAN

After hearing a presentation at a conference, high school principal Mr. Miller has banned all Web 2.0 tools, including Facebook, Skype, YouTube, wikis, blogs, and Flickr. A number of teachers and many students are upset with this decision, but Mr. Miller cites federal law as a legal reason for blocking the sites.

SOCIAL NETWORKING SCENARIO 5: THE BLOG ABOUT BLOBS

PE teacher Mr. Teng has created a widely read blog about teaching elementary physical education and health. In one post he describes (but does not name) several students and teachers he sees as having poor eating habits that contribute to their having an unhealthy BMI score, and he uses the term "blobs" to describe them. One teacher thinks he is writing about her and brings the post to the attention of the principal.

Some Online Writing Guidelines for Teachers

I enjoy being somewhat subversive when writing in my personal blog. Like many educational bloggers, I am discontented with current educational practices and trumpet change. But I also have to be careful writing as a critic.

When I first started teaching back in the mid-1970s, the district for which I worked expected teachers to set a "moral" example. And the good folks in central Iowa had a pretty rigid definition of moral. Not being able to drink a beer on my own front porch rankled me then, and it rankles me today to think that my free speech rights might be abrogated if I were banned from blogging.

But I remind myself that rights are always accompanied by responsibilities.

Here are some things I try to keep in mind when I blog. I really don't want *Johnson v. Board of Education* being studied in school law one day.

- **Write assuming your boss is reading.** That's good advice as far as it goes. But I know my wife, my mother, and my daughter all read my blog too. I assume my coworkers read the blog, as might anyone for whom I might work someday. Knowing this forces me to ask questions about language, taste, and approach.

- **Gripe globally; praise locally.** I don't think anyone really fusses if I express my opinion about global warming, the economy, or politics. But you will never catch me dissing a person who lives near enough that he could come by and TP my house. I'd just as soon not have to avoid anyone at conferences. I keep my complaints about ideas, not people.

- **Write for edited publications.** I've been writing for print publications for over twenty years. My bosses have even shared things I've written with the school board. Were the district now to react negatively to my blog, it would have a difficult case showing that my writing disrupts the workplace because it has not done so in the past.

- **Write out of goodness.** I have a difficult time believing that anything sincerely written to improve education, kids' lives, or society will be counted against a person. Writing to vent, to whine, or to ridicule will cause problems. In schools, where dismissing someone for performance is nearly impossible, supervisors are often looking for any means of firing people. If you are doing a good job at work, blog; if you aren't, don't.

Every educator should share his or her ideas. It is our professional duty to share what works for us and ask for help when we are stymied. Blogs and other online tools allow us to do both, and it would be a crying shame if fear stopped this flow of information.

Write and share, fellow educators. And be a little subversive.

CHAPTER EIGHT

Developing a Long-Term Learning Strategy

Now, here, you see, it takes all the running you can do, to keep in the same place. If you want to get somewhere else, you must run at least twice as fast as that!

—*Lewis Carroll*

The ancient Chinese supposedly had this curse: "May you live in interesting times." For those of us in education, these are interesting times indeed. Technology, education, and society itself all seem to be changing at a pace with which few of us can keep up. Like those poor inhabitants of Alice's looking-glass world, we are running as fast as we can just to keep in the same place.

"Continuing education" prior to Internet connectivity and the rapid rate of change it brought about consisted of reading professional journals, attending professional conferences, completing school-based in-service programs, and taking college classes. These activities are still available and important. But given the pace and amount of change, they alone are insufficient to keep most of us current with the happenings in education, let alone in educational technology.

Thank goodness for these online continuing education options:

- Electronic mailing lists (also known as listservs) continue to be a valuable means of locating "primary source" information—human expertise. Nearly every professional organization runs a mailing list for its members, often at both national and state levels. A simple query to the hundreds or thousands of subscribers to such lists often results not only in recommended published information but also in shared experiences and wisdom.

Survival tip: Some mailing lists archive their messages for later retrieval. A quick search may offer some answers to commonly asked questions.

- Smaller "professional networks," such as Ning sites, are complementing mailing lists by providing a forum for discussion along with a means of sharing photos, videos, and other resources with fellow network members. Aimed at creating links for professionals, these sites created for specific professions or interests operate much like the larger networking sites Facebook and LinkedIn.

- Blogs and their aural and visual cousins, podcasts and vidcasts, let teachers read or hear about, react to, and converse on the latest thinking by leaders in education. Information on blogs tends to be timely, and concise, and opinionated. Pick the blogs that are fun to read, use your RSS feed aggregator to track them, and you, like me, will become addicted.

- Webcasts, presentations, and workshops done via an Internet Web site like GoToMeeting, WebEx, or Elluminate are becoming increasingly popular. Watch your e-mail from professional associations, schools, and businesses for notices about these "webinars."

- Finally, multi-user virtual environments (MUVEs), such as Second Life, are offering a growing number of opportunities to interact and learn with colleagues. Your Second Life avatar can attend a presentation, communicate with fellow professionals in real time, and even build virtual learning resources using this powerful information and communication interface.

These are just a few of the growing number of "continuous learning" opportunities the Internet is making available to those of us engaged in the rapidly evolving field of education.

Survival tip: Many state and national professional organizations have aggressively moved into providing opportunities for teacher training online. Subscribe to their mailing lists and electronic newsletters to keep informed.

Does your school's mission statement include the words "lifelong learning"? It should. And the sentiment should also apply to us as well as our students.

Keeping Your Sanity

If you are a classroom teacher who wants to take advantage of powerful technologies for use in your classroom and for other professional tasks—but still have time to talk to your own family, read a book, or even get some sleep—consider the following strategies:

1. **Start with the problem, not the tool.** Rather than scan the flood of "new and recommended" programs, apps, and Web sites for things that look cool or useful, start with two or three challenges you have in your work life. Do you have a unit that doesn't engage your students? Are you having a problem getting a project done with your curriculum team? Is it frustrating keeping files current among the multiple devices you use? What might help meet the objectives of your professional learning community? Scan for tools that help solve real problems.

2. **Be selective about where you get your recommendations.** Let's face it, there are folks who get excited about anything that is new, shiny, and beeps. For those who want to make trying out new technology resources their avocation and forgo any attempt at normalcy, that's great. But I would select two or three trusted sources of new programs. These sources might be Web sites or blogs, your librarian or tech integration specialist, or a fellow teacher. But let somebody else do a prescreening of all the new stuff.

3. **Try just one new tool at a time.** Trying to learn too many programs can be as destructive to your professional life as ignoring technology completely. Pick one interesting resource and use it for a month. Then try another one. Nobody has to be the master of every technology available.

4. **One in, one out.** When I buy a new pair of shoes, I throw an old pair away. (This drives my wife crazy.) When I start to read a new blog, I unsubscribe from an old blog. If you create an online Web page for parents, stop doing the printed newsletter. Figuring out what to *stop* doing is probably the hardest but most important thing you need to do to stay sane.

5. **Don't try to fix that which is not broken.** If you are happy with your Web browser, your online bookmarking site, your cloud-based photo storage space, your blogging software, and your e-mail system, stay with them. Change for the sake of change is unproductive.

6. **Weigh the time-benefit ratio.** Evaluate the new resource as objectively as possible. Will taking two hours to master this program save you more than two hours in time in the immediate future? Will it help you reach students who could not be reached before? Let's face it—some programs are too complex and too time-intensive to learn to ever offer a decent payback. Evaluate.

7. **Give back and become part of a community of learners.** Be your school's guru on one helpful tool. Join a group of other technology-learning educators either face-to-face or online. Make learning new technologies social, and make friends. After all, misery does love company.

Striving for balance is the key to keeping your sanity in times of rapid change. You do not have to know everything, try everything, change everything—just work on the things that make a real and positive difference.

Your insanity may be temporary.

The Librarian: Your Technology Partner

One of my favorite movie scenes is from *Butch Cassidy and the Sundance Kid*. A posse traps Butch and Sundance on a ledge high above a river. They realize they will need to "take the leap" if they are to avoid capture. When Sundance confesses that he can't swim, Butch gives him one end of his belt to grip and they finally jump together. (This was before it was acceptable for cowboys to hold hands.)

Having a partner in any enterprise that seems risky lessens the fear factor and improves one's chance of success. When you are implementing a new project that uses technology, I wholeheartedly recommend that you ask your librarian to be your "technology partner." You will find that today's best library media specialists (LMSs) have

1. **A healthy attitude toward technology.** The LMS considers and teaches not just how to use technology but also why and under what circumstances it should be used. (A sexist syllogism: most librarians are women. Women have a healthier attitude toward technology than do men. Therefore most librarians have a healthy attitude toward technology.) If using traditional methods or resources will work better, a LMS will say so.

2. **Good teaching skills.** Unlike technicians, LMSs are more likely to use good pedagogical techniques and communication skills because they are trained teachers. Librarians are understanding and empathetic when technology-related stress occurs in the classroom.

3. **An understanding of the use of technology in the process of gaining information literacy and in fostering higher-level thinking skills.** Librarians view technology as just one more, extremely powerful tool that can be used by students completing well-designed information literacy projects. Many technology specialists are just now realizing that using information technologies to solve problems and answer questions is more powerful than using these tools simply as electronic workbooks.

4. **Experience as skill integrators and collaborators.** Integration of research and information literacy projects has been a long-term goal of school library programs, and as a result many LMSs have become excellent collaborators with classroom teachers, successfully strengthening the classroom curriculum. They are interested less in integrating technology than in improving your lessons. Librarians know kids, know technology, know what works, *and* know how to work with others.

5. **Been models for the successful use of technology.** The library's automated library catalogs, circulation systems, electronic reference materials, and student-accessible workstations all showed up well before classroom technologies. The general-use computer lab in a building is often in or adjacent to the library. This means that the LMS is often the educator with the most comfort with technology in your school.

6. **Provided in-building support.** Even a semi-flexibly scheduled LMS can work with you in the library, lab, or classroom. Unlike another classroom teacher or a district technology person, the LMS is available for questions that might otherwise derail your project *when you need him or her*. Having ready support just down the hall is critical to any technology project.

7. **A whole-school view.** Next to the principal, the LMS has the most inclusive view of the school and its resources. The librarian knows what is available, where it is, and how to get more. Need a second digital camera? Hmm, the second-grade classrooms aren't using theirs just now ...

8. **Concerns about the ethical use of technology.** Students will need to have the skills to self-evaluate information; understand online copyright laws and intellectual property issues; and follow the rules of safety and appropriate use of resources. Who but the librarian worries about this stuff and can help you understand its complexities as well? Parents will want to know that you've been working to make sure their children are safe, ethical users of technology.

Whether you feel comfortable enough to hold hands or not, look to your library media specialist when taking your next big technology "leap."

My New (School) Year's Resolutions

Around the first of August each year I start to miss "school." In June and July, the (relatively) empty buildings, (relatively) quiet telephones, and (relatively) low volume of e-mail are a welcome relief. But by early August I get lonesome and excited about staff and students returning. And every year I resolve to try a few new things that will improve my technology use, my teaching abilities, and, ideally, the lives of my students and staff.

My new school year resolutions include the following:

- **I will learn one new piece of software or hardware so well that I can teach its use to others.**

    Mastering any piece of software or equipment is deceptively difficult and time consuming. But most of us can learn each year *one* new program or device well enough to make it useful to us and to teach it to others.

- **I will read at least four or five "big idea" books and try to put some ideas from them into my professional practice.**

    These are not necessarily books on technology or even education per se, but books about ideas that may well have a significant impact on education, technology, and my fellow teachers' and students' lives. Or, hey, an impact on *my* life!

- **I will identify and revise my three least satisfactory lessons.**

    It's pretty easy to keep teaching lessons without making significant changes. If something has been even moderately successful in the past, why take the time, effort, and *risk* involved in changing it? But I am increasingly discovering that my best workshops are the ones not only with the best content but also with the most engaging activities that allow participants to apply and practice ideas—not just hear about them. Sure, there's a chance an activity will bomb, but there's an even better chance it will make the workshop better.

    Revisions that purposely include technology are among my best. Whether I am using a response system to get participant input; conducting real-time, online surveys; or just adding materials for participants to use on my workshop wiki, technology is playing an important role in my best workshops.

- **I will try one new communication strategy.**

    Where do your students "live" online? What are their parents' preferred means of communication? How do you get and keep the attention of your administrator?

Students are rapidly shifting from e-mailing to texting and Facebook messaging as their primary means of communication. How many of your parents may look at text messages or "tweets" who don't look at the printed newsletter that may or may not make it home with their children? Would a multimedia presentation convince your principal in a way a memo might not?

- **I will attempt to learn one new human relations skill.**

    Maybe this should have been my first resolution. Each year seems to bring big technology changes in our district. The new mail server, a big installation of interactive whiteboards, greater use of data-mining software, new operating systems, different supplementary software for our math textbook series, and ever-growing expectations of teachers and administrators all will cause stress around here. I know much of my job will be to learn how to deal with *others'* stress.

    Gandhi's famous admonition, "You must be the change you want to see in the world," is especially true for educators. Better schools start with each of us improving each year. Resolve to "be the change" each new school year.

Bonus: Top Ten Secrets for Conducting a Successful Technology Workshop

Congratulations! Because of your recognized expertise in an area—gained through research, study, or practice—*you* have been selected to give a workshop to your peers! This is just the first step toward celebrity status in the education world. Your own line of designer clothes, a private jet, and fawning fans will soon follow. Start thinking now about how to avoid the paparazzi!

Sorry, got carried away.

As a veteran workshop presenter, workshop attendee, and high school speech teacher, I'd like to offer ten suggestions on what makes a superb experience for both the participants and *you*. Advice is on the left and an ongoing example is on the right.

1. Know your role.

The focus of a good workshop is on building basic understandings, teaching key concepts, and allowing for practice of some useful skills. Think of yourself as a workbook, not a textbook. The real genius of most great workshops is the presenter's ability to take a complex topic and make it understandable and useful rather than to give in-depth "coverage" or to display his or her commanding mastery of a topic. In writing, Stephen Jay Gould has done this with science, making difficult concepts understandable to the layperson. Take a good look at the strategies used by the *For Dummies* series: lots of lists, lots of analogies, and an emphasis on the practical.

You can and should build participants' confidence by being approachable and giving them respect—not through overwhelming them with factoids, three-letter acronyms, and long, detailed background information. Do not draw attention to small errors that you might make during the workshop. ("Gee, I see I made a really stupid spelling error on this slide" or "I guess I forgot to include that in the handouts.") Trust me, nobody notices these sorts of things until *you* point them out. People really do want presenters who know what they are doing—or at least appear to.

2. Limit your topic.

Although it is counterintuitive, your biggest problem will *not* be finding enough to talk about but rather limiting what you will present. You have a topic—now take time to determine the three or four key understandings or skills you want people to leave feeling they have down cold. Remember, your goal is to empower, not overpower.

Gee, I've really been doing a lot with digital photography both at home and at school. I've read up on it, I've reapplied some of my training in 35 mm photography to digital photography, and some of the things I've done with digital photography in school have been effective. I think I'll do a workshop for the next teacher conference!

I know not everyone is as into photography as I am, but there are some pretty simple ways everyone can both improve the quality of a digital picture and use digital photography in teaching. I'll assume people have a fairly inexpensive camera, limited editing software, and lots of other things to do in the classroom besides using photographs. Let's call the workshop: It's a Snap! Making the Most of Digital Photography in Your Classroom.

So, then, here are my goals:
1. *Help participants understand how powerful visuals are in teaching, especially with this generation of learners.*
2. *Teach some simple techniques for taking and editing digital photos.*

3. Be organized and communicate that organization.

Your key understandings or skills should be your presentation's organization road map, with each understanding or skill building on the previous one. Although it is important that you know where you are going, it is just as critical that your participants know this as well. In your talk, slides, and handouts, use this map to help both you and your participants stay focused. As you move from one understanding or skill to the next, take a moment to review the previous understandings. A graphic representation of this map is very helpful for most participants (because there are more visual learners than meet the eye). This can be as simple as three or four different-color text boxes repeated throughout your slides or as complex as a computer-generated concept map.

4. Set out a problem or possibility, then offer a solution or opportunity.

Obviously you think the information and skills you are teaching are important to the participants. Do *they* know that? Don't assume so. One masterful way to develop both interest and attention is to start with a seemingly insolvable problem or terrific opportunity and then show how your workshop will help folks solve that problem or take advantage of that opportunity.

3. Show some ways a teacher can use digital images in materials created for students, and suggest some simple projects students can do with digital cameras.

The map for my presentation:

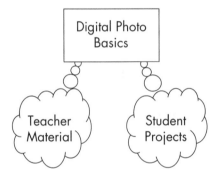

My introduction . . . hmmm, let's see.

1. I think I'll pose these questions: "Do you have students who don't seem to pay attention? Do you have students who have a hard time understanding concepts through reading? Would you like a quick and easy way to integrate technology in your classroom and give students practice in a new form of communication?"

A short check at the beginning of your talk about the composition of your attendees will help you ingeniously "customize" your workshop on the fly. The examples you use might differ if your group is mostly librarians, mostly technologists, mostly classroom teachers, or mostly administrators—or they might vary according to the level of expertise the group already has with a technology.

The short check can be as easy as simply asking at the beginning of the talk, "How many of you in here are classroom teachers (librarians, technologists, and so on)?" Another good way to get to know your group is by asking an open-ended question about your topic. "What are the biggest difficulties your students face in doing good research?" or "Why don't some students read voluntarily?" or "What problems do you encounter when trying to do digital photography?"

2. *Then I will ask participants to complete a short checklist on using digital cameras and photos, and I will ask them to share how they did.*

Survival tip: An accurate program description that clearly states whether a session is for beginners or advanced computer users will help narrow the range of skills that must be accommodated in a workshop.

5. Be conversational and have fun.

You do not have to be a powerful orator to be a good workshop presenter. In fact, a formal speaking style will work against you. Instead, envision yourself in your living room visiting with a group of good friends, and use the same conversational approach you would use there. Build a human connection between you and your group, whether it is five people or five hundred. Even if you have been given an introduction by a room host, take about three minutes (no longer) to let the participants know you are actually a human being—a brief summary of your career, an experience that got you interested in the topic, or some other personal connection with the topic. (Oh, the old advice to picture your audience naked does *not* work. Depending on who is in the front row you will either be so aroused or grossed out you won't be able to concentrate.) Think about stories you can share that help you make your points clearly and effectively. All great teachers are basically effective storytellers. The concrete examples create interest and provide experiences to which the participants can relate, and stories will build that human connection.

Finally, remember that if you are not having fun, nobody else is either. A good laugh, either intentional or unintentional, that comes as a result of a comment by you or a participant is a very good thing. Humor helps create that vital affective bond between presenter and participant.

I'll try to add some fun and humanize myself by . . .

1. *Using some family photos as samples to practice editing*

2. *Making sure I tell about the project Stacie did in my class that included a picture of her mom in her bathrobe and her dad drinking a beer*

3. *Showing some examples of my own bad photos and how I improved them*

6. Use good handouts and good slides that complement rather than duplicate.

In Secret 1 I suggested that you should consider yourself the workbook, not the textbook. This is not to dismiss the fact that attendees may want detailed, complex materials for further study. Your handouts can provide that information through reprinted articles (with permission), annotated bibliographies, links to Web sites, or detailed charts and graphs.

> **Survival tip:** Rather than making paper copies of your handouts, put them online in a wiki or on a Web page. That way they can be kept up-to-date and easily shared. And you'll waste fewer resources.

A great use for handouts is as a guide to the activities that will be described in the next section of the presentation. My thoughts on good PowerPoint use are summed up in Chapter Three, so I won't repeat them here. Succinctly, there should be a compelling reason for a slide to exist. It needs to contain a short key point, movie, graphic, discussion question, or activity prompt. Slides should *not* contain the entire text of your presentation so you can simply read them. I've seen too many presenters do just that, and I just want to dope slap 'em. Less is more. Do think about this: the visuals on your slides can be highly affective as well as cognitively informative. By association, your believability (and likeability) will increase if you use photographs of happy, smiling students or teachers. For that artistic look, run them through a filter in an editing program. As suggested earlier, a graphic road map helps organize your participants.

My handouts will include

1. *A bibliography and links to some good sources about choosing a digital camera and about visual literacy and learners, a primer on good photo taking, a link to some videos on photo editing, and a list of popular digital editing programs*

2. *Activities I will be doing with the participants during the workshop, including critiquing a photo, cropping a photo, brainstorming ways to use digital photos in my lessons, and creating a project in my curriculum that asks students to use digital photos*

3. *Examples of a student handout, a lesson supported by photographs I've taken, and a letter to parents that included digital photos*

4. *Lesson plans with assessment tools that have been used successfully in my school*

My slides will include

1. *My organization road map*

2. *My major points and discussion questions as well as instructions for the activities*

3. *Examples of photographs to critique*

4. *Examples of photographs before and after editing*

5. *Examples of student projects that have used student-produced photos*

6. *Photos of my kids working with cameras and editing software (included on all slides)*

7. Less talk, more action.

I know without a doubt that I am never bored when *I* am the one doing the talking. I can't say the same for those attending my workshops, so I try to give them every opportunity to do things other than simply listen. I once had a professional speech coach suggest to me that one should never go for more than twenty minutes without an activity that involves the participants. These "activities" can be as simple as "Share with your neighbor two ways . . ." or "Jot down one way you might use this idea in your classroom" or "Everyone stand up and repeat after me . . ." The idea is to get minds out of neutral and into gear and to stimulate discussion. Other, more formal activities (which I always ask be done in small groups) include taking a short quiz, doing an Edward de Bono PMI (Plus-Minus-Interesting) decision-making activity, or filling out a bubble diagram in a handout. If you direct questions to the whole group, make the questions both easy and open-ended. Questions calling for a "correct" response make you sound like the teacher in *Ferris Bueller's Day Off*.

Oh, activities are a great way to control the length of your workshop. If the workshop is running long, don't give participants much time to do them; if the workshop is running short, allow more time. Classes that take place in computer labs should be nearly all hands-on. Small groups tend to be more productive than individuals in labs, I also find. Oh, and give people a break for goodness sake, somewhere after about an hour and fifteen minutes. Presenters more clever than I have designed activities that get people standing or moving around. The mind can only absorb as much as the butt can tolerate, right?

Activities:

1. *I'll give the opening quiz.*

2. *I'll ask, "Who is the worst photographer in your family and why?"*

3. *I'll ask participants (in pairs) to critique a photo and offer advice on how it should be edited.*

4. *I'll ask participants to brainstorm at least three ways they can use digital photos in their own instructional and communication practices.*

5. *I'll have teams of participants pick a curricular unit and design a project that asks students to use digital photos.*

6. *If I have a lab and this is a full-day workshop, I will ask participants to practice cropping, eliminating red-eye, and "enhancing" a photo they have taken.*

8. Give participants a chance to practice, apply, and reflect.

The best workshops are ones that not only introduce me to new ideas but also reassure me about my current practices. Send folks away with some "low-hanging fruit"—very simple suggestions for things they can implement the next day back in school. And finally, allow some time for participants to reflect on their own practices. How often does that happen on the job? Great workshops are the ones that feel more like a conversation than a lecture. If I, as the workshop leader, don't learn something from the participants about the topic, I have not been successful. It is amazing what good ideas participants bring with them, and getting them to share those ideas with the group is an important part of your job. Although I dislike the term *facilitator,* it happens to be just the right word in this case. So, then, you give people a chance to discuss and what happens? Somebody makes an off-topic or hostile comment or asks a question from far-left field. Or somebody sets out to show that he or she (almost always a *he*) knows just a whole heck of a lot more than you do about this particular topic. The trick is to both ignore and honor those folks and never get rattled, angry, or defensive. Practice responses like these:

- "That sounds like something that I need to do more thinking about myself."
- "That's a great question, and I'm afraid we'd need a whole other workshop to answer it."
- "Gee, what does the rest of the group think?"

Of course you can always break down in copious weeping, but you will still need to go on with the workshop eventually.

I will remember to use my activities, and, when we are critiquing photographs, I will make sure the participants are the ones offering the suggestions.

I'm sure my "Create a photographic time line of your Saturday" will be a project everyone will feel she or he can do with students.

Most participants will also appreciate the simple tips I'll give for improving their picture taking. (I'd better remember to put in the description of the session that the workshop is for beginners!)

9. End with a summary, on an upbeat note, and on time.

At the end, repeat your initial goals for the workshop and quickly summarize the main ideas. As I used to teach my speech kids:

- Tell'm what you're going to tell'm.
- Tell'm.
- Then tell'm what you just told'm.

Your last remarks should offer a charge to your group to apply the skills they've just learned. A little inspiration or a humorous quote brings closure. Say thanks and give participants a way to contact you with follow-up questions. Ask the nice ones to fill out the session evaluation form. And, this might be the most important factor of all, end on time or even a little early. I have yet to hear a single complaint about a workshop that ended at 3:45 instead of 4:00. In fact, a cheap way to be very popular is to make sure you end early enough for your group to be first in the lunch line, at the exhibits, or in the bar. Ending more than five minutes late is criminal under any circumstances and may qualify as torture under the rules of the Geneva Convention.

10. I'm letting you out early. See above. Any complaints?

This is easy. Using my graphic road map, I'll summarize the major points I talked about:

1. *"Visuals can help students learn, and students like communicating visually. Digital photography makes that easy."*

2. *"Remember the simple photo-taking skills I suggested and some editing techniques."*

3. *"We looked at some ways that you can use photographs in teaching and communicating."*

4. *"Think about where you can give students a chance to use photos they've taken to communicate." I'll encourage them to start simple and to know that every project gets better. How's this for an ending quote? "Treat your students as you do your pictures, and place them in their best light" (paraphrased from Jennie Churchill). I'll remind the group that my e-mail address is in my handouts.*

CHAPTER NINE

Looking into the Crystal Ball

The future is already here—it's just not very evenly distributed.

—*William Gibson*

Futurists have a bad track record—just watch any science fiction movie from the 1950s or 1960s and try to find a computer screen, a digital clock, or even an interstate highway cloverleaf. I grew up reading predictions of hovercraft cars, meals in a pill, and robot servants. Instead, we have the Internet, solar power, and nanotechnologies. Who knew?

The New Media Consortium has been publishing a short document called *The Horizon Report* annually since 2004 and *The Horizon Report: K–12 Edition* annually since 2009. These publications, compiled by a panel of experts in the educational technology field, predict what technology devices, applications, and trends will have the biggest impact on schools and schooling.

Most of their predictions have underestimated the time it has taken for new technologies to reach K–12 education and overestimated the technologies' impact on how schooling has actually changed as a result. Ubiquitous wireless technologies, social networking, "extended learning," gaming, virtual worlds, smartphones, augmented reality, and sophisticated search tools have all appeared in a number of their reports. Some of these technologies have indeed made it into K–12 schools, but they have done so on a limited basis and have had a limited impact on teaching and learning in the typical classroom.

The reports have also missed a few technologies that *are* having an impact on schools: cloud-based productivity tools, online testing, data-mining applications, and parent portals to their children's progress.

So it is with trepidation that I offer the "futuristic" scenarios viewed in my cracked and cloudy crystal ball.

Three "High-Tech" Schools of the Future

These three future scenarios, each extending a current trend, reflect different philosophies about the purposes of education and how technology can be used to fulfill those purposes. While reading, ask yourself which future your school might be heading toward. How might better, alternative future schools use technology to meet their goals?

SKINNER ELEMENTARY SCHOOL

Sixth grader Carla's inner-city school has a one-to-one ratio of computer workstations to students. And Carla spends about four hours each day at a computer.

The primary goal of Carla's elementary school is to make sure all students pass state and federal tests in reading, mathematics, and writing. Instruction in the "basic skills" is provided by carefully designed courseware that offers short tutorials using a variety of media, frequent assessments, and remedial instruction incorporating several approaches. At the end of each school day, Carla's progress is summarized and sent automatically to the school's assessment office, where it is monitored—along with the daily reports of the other six hundred students at Skinner Elementary.

Carla, along with half of the student body, uses the school's computer labs for four hours a day—from 8:05 AM to 12:05 PM, and these four hours are the only time Carla is in school.* At 12:35 PM the other half of the student body uses the computer labs. There are three large labs that contain one hundred workstations each. The courseware is the only program available on the student workstations. The lab is staffed by four paraprofessionals who help Carla if her computer is having problems. There are also two certified teachers in the building who are available when a paraprofessional can't answer a question.

Carla is a good student, but she struggled with fractions. When the daily report showed this, Carla was scheduled for special remedial instruction. Carla met with a certified special education teacher for an hour a week. This teacher provided a small device that had special software dedicated to practicing fractions. Carla caught up quickly.

Doing well is important to Carla. At regular assembly programs, students are recognized for high percentages of right answers, good attendance, and especially good behavior. Although she does not do it herself, Carla knows most of the kids in her class bring their smartphones to class and use them to text each other and read popular books and magazines, despite this being strictly forbidden.

---

*Parents are responsible for child care outside the four hours students are in school. Whereas Carla goes home and cares for her younger brother and sister until her parents come home from work, other students take part in latchkey programs organized by the YMCA and local churches.

Carla appears to be on track for graduation from elementary school and is looking forward to beginning the technical school track at the nearby middle school in the fall.

Skinner Elementary is often singled out as an exemplary school because such a high percentage of students meet state and national testing goals and because it operates on about 80 percent of the funding of "traditional" schools. (The school saves money by not providing a hot lunch program; a library; art, music, or physical education classes; or a playground.)

JOHN DEWEY HIGH SCHOOL

Carlos's mobile is behaving strangely. And it's a bad time for this to happen because one of his biggest projects is due on Friday. Project-based learning is the core of Carlos's "magnet" high school education.

On the four days he attends school,** Carlos spends the majority of his time in the "learning commons"—a huge room that contains groupings of tables, chairs, and soft seating. Carlos also has a personal workspace he rarely uses. Meeting with his learning groups, Carlos spends his time in school completing multidisciplinary, collaborative projects. He does meet at least twice a week with his adviser in a classroom setting, but primarily he is working, both online and face-to-face, with one of his learning teams.

The projects that form the core of Carlos's schoolwork are carefully designed to ensure that state standards are addressed, that the work is relevant to Carlos, and that his work is authentically assessed. For students to become "self-assessing" learners is a major goal at Dewey High.

Carlos likes using a lightweight tablet mobile with a ten-inch touch screen as his personal communication and creation device. He is literally never without it, and the school is fully wireless. Other students prefer laptops, smartphones, or netbooks, but the purpose is the same—to access peers, teachers, resources, and their own work. Due to the individualized nature of learning at the school, textbooks have all but disappeared, and those remaining are electronic and leveled. Dewey High also has some computers that are more powerful for such complex tasks as video editing and producing graphics.

Carlos loves school and works hard, but his mother, who is an electrical engineer and member of the parent advisory council, has concerns. She worries that her son's coursework lacks the rigor that he'll need when he reaches college. In fact, performance on state and national tests and participation in AP classes is below average at Dewey High, and colleges report a high percentage of freshmen needing

---

**At the high school level the school's custodial responsibilities are less important.

remedial math and writing classes. Other parents worry that graduates won't have the common basics of historical, literary, and scientific information.

DUNCAN MIDDLE SCHOOL

Carl watches carefully as his language arts teacher uses the interactive whiteboard (IWB) to show the relationship between a subject and its pronoun. He knows that he may be expected to demonstrate his mastery of the concept at the IWB himself. Although the subject itself is not that interesting, Carl watches carefully and believes he has grasped the concept.

A few of Carl's teachers are using technology in the classroom in interesting ways. In social studies last year, his class adopted a sister school in Singapore and did a joint online problem-solving exercise that included a Skype video call; Carl still has a couple of Singaporean students as Facebook friends from the experience. Math class uses calculators that are networked with the IWB. The same math teacher regularly records a lesson so it can be viewed multiple times on a video streaming site. In health class, the teacher spiced things up in the human sexuality unit by having students respond to a poll using "clickers."

Now and then the principal and another strange-looking person (who Carl later finds out is the technology director) bring visitors into classrooms to watch these technology-infused lessons. On its Web site the school touts a "cutting-edge, high-tech environment that builds 21st-century skills."

When students do use technology in school, it is most often when writing papers in the lab attached to the library or conducting research using the school's one set of laptops that travel in a cart—at least when those computers aren't being used during the six formal testing periods each school year. Last year a teacher wrote a grant and received funding for small touch screen devices that the kids used for a couple weeks to complete a science activity.

Although some technologies are used and used well at Duncan Middle School, too often Carl's teachers give lectures accompanied by dull, wordy slide shows; his school still uses print textbooks; and photocopied worksheet completion is a daily expectation. Carl's backpack weighs thirty pounds. Although there is no schoolwide ban on the use of personal mobile devices, most of Carl's teachers will confiscate them if they see students using them during class. However, statewide budget cuts have resulted in average class sizes of over forty students, so texting during class usually goes undetected. Most kids use their own mobiles and Internet connections in school because the most popular social networking sites are blocked by the school's filter.

When Carl starts a class, he really doesn't know how or if the teacher will be using technology—there are no common expectations except that all teachers will use the district's electronic grade book and attendance program. Technology is not a part of the district's strategic plan, its curriculum development, or staff development efforts.

Despite large sums of money being spent on hardware, infrastructure, and support, technology seems to be having little impact on either improving test scores or accomplishing the other goals of the school. In this way, Duncan Middle School has changed very little over the past twenty years.

SO WHAT'S THE POINT?

The best way to predict the future is to invent it.

—Alan Kay

It's really tough to be "for" or "against" technology in schools. As you can tell from the preceding examples, "technology in schools" means different things to different people. In each scenario there are aspects that most of us would like and aspects that we might dislike—or even find frightening or inhumane.

Skinner Elementary School has a single, focused mission: to get as many kids to pass tests at the lowest cost possible. And technology allows it to do this. At John Dewey High School, technology is a tool for helping create problem solvers, team workers, and independent learners. Duncan Middle School teachers use technology to engage students and enhance traditional teaching practices.

Yet each school also has problems. Skinner Elementary ignores most child development needs and treats children like robots. Dewey High cannot satisfy parents or the state that its program provides sufficient rigor and meets standards. And although some Duncan Middle School teachers provide "pockets of wow," technology has no quantifiable impact on the mission of the school or the success of the students.

In which school would you want to teach? Which school would you want your children or grandchildren to attend? With which school would you be most proud to be associated?

What model will be the school of the future?

How You Can Invent the Future and Take Charge of Your Own Technology Environment

The biggest mistake teachers can make in regard to technology use is to simply let the future happen to them rather than be a serious part of creating their own future. But how do you do this as a teacher and still have time to teach?

That's what the rest of this chapter will explore—how to determine your own technology future. Here are six ways you can take charge today:

HAVE A PERSONAL VISION OF EDUCATION AND HOW TECHNOLOGY SHOULD BE USED IN IT

One of my favorite recipes for change is this simply stated formula: $C = V \times D \times F > R$. Richard Beckhard and David Gleicher posit that **C**hange = **V**ision × **D**iscontent × **F**irst steps > **R**esistance. Both vision and discontent are in plentiful supply in most schools and communities. It's figuring out how to develop a shared vision and then get the resources needed to make those first steps toward making it come true that is lacking.

Teachers who invent their own future take time to reflect, to formulate a personal vision of what education ought to look like, and to consider the role technology plays in that vision. And then they modify what they do, even slightly, to move toward that educational model.

My Personal Predictions About Technology in Schools

Know what's weird? Day by day, nothing seems to change, but pretty soon . . . everything's different. —*Calvin from* Calvin and Hobbes

I always try to practice what I preach, so these are my personal predictions about technology and education.

In the future . . .

1. There will be less emphasis on "technology" as a separate area of concern and more emphasis on technology as a means to achieve goals in other areas. There will also be a greater need for procedures that allow for joint decision making among all technology users.

2. There will be a greater need to train students and staff on ethics, safety, and civility when using technology, as well as to train them to evaluate the reliability of information found and to use it purposefully.

3. Schools will experience a greater need for a secure source of adequate technology funding. They will strategize to decrease "total cost of ownership" through maintenance outsourcing, using thin client architectures, having staff and students adopt handheld computers, and purchasing upgradeable devices. There will also be greater accountability for technology expenditures and for the impact of technologies on school effectiveness.

4. Parents will increasingly desire real-time student information available via the Web. There will be higher parent expectations of schools and teachers to provide

comprehensive information about school programs and individual student achievement.

5. The (technology-based) tools and knowledge needed to do good data-driven planning and decision making by administrators, building teams, and individual teachers will be of increased importance.

6. Technology skills will continue to be integrated into the content areas to meet specific state and national standards, leading to increased demand for individualized technology training by staff. There will also be an increase in the use of software designed to help low-achieving students and English language learners learn state-tested skills.

7. There will be a continued, accelerated move toward information in digital formats, such as e-books, online databases, Web-based videoconferences, and video on demand. Individual teachers will increasingly be able to create and make available materials accessible from the Web. There will be more capacity for electronically shared and submitted student work.

8. There will be increased efforts to ensure data privacy, data security, and network reliability.

9. Increased educational options for all learners will include more choices of schools, more online course offerings, more interactive video offerings, and more computer courseware options. This will result in an increased need for school marketing efforts and more "consumer-driven" choices made by school officials.

10. There will be an accelerated blending of "technology integration specialists" and school "library media specialists" into a single job that takes responsibility for the instructional and curricular uses of technology, supported by more narrowly defined district-level positions of network managers, technicians, and student information system managers.

11. In-school use of student-owned technologies including cell phones, PDAs, and laptops will increase. Most of these will connect wirelessly to each other and to the Internet, creating new security and ethical challenges. There will be more emphasis on anytime, anyplace access to personal information through Web-based personal file space, calendars, and wirelessly networked handheld devices. The "digital divide" will shrink due to inexpensive cell phones with Internet access.

12. Continued "bare-bones" funding of states' educational systems will force schools to make tough program choices. If programs can't quantitatively demonstrate that they make a difference in achievement, they and the people in them will be subject to the budget axe.

13. There will be increased efforts to ensure all teachers use technology to improve teaching and learning at least at a minimum level through improved teacher review processes that include criteria for technology use.

Now, I am cheating here just a little. I actually made these predictions as a part of a technology plan I wrote in 2003. I'm still waiting for the day "everything's different."

HAVE A VOICE IN SCHOOL TECHNOLOGY POLICYMAKING AND PLANNING

I often hear comments like this from teachers who are upset about the technology policies in their district:

"They" are blocking school access to YouTube.

"They" make us use PCs when I'd rather have a Mac.

"They" won't let me access my grade book from home.

"They" won't let me use my personal laptop computer on the school's network.

"They" insist we have long and complicated passwords and make us change them all the time.

The question I have when I hear statements like these is: "Just who is this mysterious 'they'?"

Can you actually name "them"? Or are "they" just a convenient scapegoat for poor policymaking procedures? Can you as a single teacher influence "them"? And are you personally working to change such decisions from being made by a faceless "they" to being made by a known "we"?

If not, you should be. It's your professional obligation.

By its very nature, policymaking is influenced by conflicting human values. Nowhere in schools is this more evident than when it comes to establishing appropriate policies for the relatively new and often confusing field of educational technology.

Larry Cuban (2001) suggests that such value conflicts present not a solvable problem but a dilemma that needs ongoing management. In other words, policymaking is an area in which there will always be conflict, no matter how hard we work to resolve issues. Disagreements about technology use have at their heart two very different sets of values, resulting in two sets of priorities—one set held by the technical staff and one by educators.

Technical people are responsible for data security, network bandwidth conservation, and the reliable operation of far too many machines. Techs desire rules that will decrease the likelihood of technical problems. Taken to the extreme, this results in an "if they can't touch it, it won't break" mentality. Allowing only limited access, overblocking, and requiring long passwords are the by-product of prioritizing security, reliability, and adequacy.

Teachers want as much access and convenience as possible. Security systems requiring multiple log-ins eat into class time, and restrictions on what is accessible and from where can discourage technology use and innovative practices. Those for whom access, convenience, and ease of use are the primary concerns often seek home access, simple passwords, private computer use, and minimal blocking.

Both parties—techs and teachers—have legitimate points of view. And both parties are interdependent. Teachers won't use the technology unless it works. Technicians are irrelevant if educators don't use technology.

There is no simple resolution to this ongoing dilemma of conflicting priorities, but I know this about making better policy decisions: the best rules and guidelines are those developed collaboratively.

District and building technology advisory committees have policy development as a major task. These small groups that meet a few times each year comprise a variety of stakeholders—teachers, librarians, administrators, students, parents, and community members, with technology personnel serving as ex officio members.

In my school district, issues raised concerning technology use are given a full hearing. I often use Edward de Bono's PMI (Plus-Minus-Interesting) tool, asking about a proposal, "What's good, what's bad, and what's interesting?" to get a constructive discussion flowing during meetings. It's a simple activity in which a statement is made (for example, "The district should allow the use of personal computers to access our wireless network"), and then small groups list the positive (+), negative (–), and interesting (?) potential consequences of the statement, with each group required to have at least one item in each column.

Collaborative policymaking can have two results: either an agreement is reached that everyone can live with; or an agreement is reached that some members don't like, but members understand why it was made. Either way, such decisions are better than those made unilaterally by a faceless "they."

> **Survival tip:** Don't let "them" make technology use less productive than it can be for you as a teacher. Find the policymakers in your school and district. If there is a technology committee in place, get on it and contribute. If there is not, lobby your administrator for the creation of one. Turn the "they" into a "we."

EXPERIMENT

Educational technology use is sufficiently new that there is not a body of "best practices" all educators should be following. The happiest and most effective teachers I know have the confidence to try new approaches to teaching and learning with technology. And they fully expect that not every experiment will work.

Survival tip: Let your principal know about your experiments, including what you are hoping to accomplish, before conducting them, and discuss what worked and what didn't work afterward. Successful technology-using teachers "monitor and adjust" during these experiments, learn from them, and then modify or discard the activities that simply are not effective.

LOOK FOR A MENTOR, COACH, OR GUIDE

Find someone in the building who is willing to teach you about new technologies. Oh, and consider that this might be a student, not an adult.

Seven Qualities of Highly Effective Technology Trainers

Here are some attributes of people who can effectively teach others to use technology. Find others in your building or district who do these things and make them your tech teachers.

1. **Always assuming the problem is on the desk, not in the chair.** When a problem arises, the best trainers assume that it is a result of a hardware or software flaw—whether an actual bug or a design in the user interface that makes the technology confusing for normal people to use—not the result of the user's stupidity. It's sometimes tough to help people increase their knowledge without making them feel stupid or incompetent, but good teachers can. Phrases like, "My third graders can do that," "You know, it works better when you plug it in," and "No, the other right arrow," are *not* recommended.

2. **Refraining from touching the learner's mouse.** Good trainers are patient. One sure sign of this saintly virtue in teachers is that they never touch a learner's mouse or keyboard. No matter how exasperating it becomes to watch that ill-coordinated person find and click on the correct button, good instructors' hands stay well behind their backs, no matter how white-knuckled they become.

3. **Having the ability to create great analogies.** There is a theory that the only way we can think about a new thing is if we have some way to relate it to what we already know. Good trainers can do that by creating analogies. "Your

e-mail account is like a post office box. Your password is like your combination to get into it. Your e-mail address is like your mailing address—it tells the electronic postmaster where to send your e-mail." Now here's the catch: truly great analogists know when the comparisons break down, too. "Unlike a human postmaster, the electronic postmaster can't make intelligent guesses about an address. A missing dot, the 'L' instead of a 'l,' or a single juxtaposition of letters will keep your mail from being delivered."

4. **Providing clear support materials.** Few things are more comforting to technology learners than being able to access a "cheat sheet" about using a new technology. Until multistep tasks are repeated several times, most of us need reminders that are more descriptive than just our notes (and more permanent than our memories). A short menu of task steps illustrated with screen shots is a gift for most technology learners.

5. **Knowing what is essential and what is only confusing.** A good trainer will have a list of the skills the learners should have mastered by the end of the training. As instruction proceeds, that list will be the basis for frequent checks for understanding. As an often random thinker, I find such a list keeps me as an instructor on track and provides a road map for the learner. Now here's the catch with this one: truly great technology teachers know what things beginning learners really need to know to make them productive and what things might be conveyed that only serve to impress a captive audience with the technologist's superior intellect. ("The e-mail address comprises the username, the domain name, the subdomain name, and the computer name, all referenced in a lookup table at the NIC." Like that.) It's an alpha wolf thing, especially common with males. Be aware of it, and look for a teacher who uses charm and a caring demeanor with the pack to achieve dominance.

6. **Assuring learners that "if it breaks, we'll fix it."** Kids catch on to technology with amazing rapidity for a very good reason. They aren't afraid to push buttons. They know if they mess something up, it's an adult's job to fix it. That's one nice thing about being a kid. However, adult learners also need the courage to experiment. Rather than always answering direct questions about technology, good trainers will often say, "Try it and see what happens. If you mess something up, I'll help you fix it."

7. **Retaining perspective.** Many of us who work with technology do so because we love it. We play with new software on the weekends, search the Internet deep into the evening, and show off our new gadgets like other folks show off prize-winning zinnias, new powerboats, or successful children. I hesitate to use the term *abnormal,* but we are in the minority.

Most teachers see technology as a sometimes helpful thing that should occupy about 1 percent of one's conscious thinking time. Good trainers who can remember what it was like before there were computers—the green grass, the singing birds, the books to read, the parties to attend, the fishing trips, the face-to-face human communication—tend to be more empathetic.

SHARE INFORMATION

Professionalism requires that practitioners share their knowledge with other practitioners. This can be done informally with fellow teachers during lunch or after school and at staff meetings. Effective practices should be shared formally . . .

- During staff and curriculum meetings
- At in-house staff development workshops
- At state and national conferences
- Through school and professional publications
- In personal blogs, "tweets," and social networking entries

Parents also like knowing about how their children are using technology in the classroom. Provided at parent-teacher conferences, in the school newsletter, and through the local media, information about interesting units that are augmented with technology is always greeted with enthusiasm.

Survival tip: If your class is doing something interesting and new with technology, call your local newspaper and television station to see if they would be interested in doing a story. The school gets good PR, and the practice may encourage others to try something similar.

SUPPORT OTHERS AND USE A TEAM-TEACHING APPROACH

Other teachers and librarians make great partners when attempting to use a new technology or an old technology for the first time. Students can also make wonderful partners for figuring out how to use a new technology when given that charge and responsibility. Don't assume that you have nothing to offer others when it comes to technology support. The applications are complex, diverse, and fast-changing. No one knows everything, but all of us know some things.

Change from the Radical Center of Education

Although the Radical Center political movement has been around for thirty years, I suggest that we who use educational technology adopt a similar view on hot-button topics. Polarized views of reading methodologies, filtering, testing, open-source software, constructivism, e-books, computer labs, different operating systems, and the one-to-one computer projects all make for entertaining reading and a raised blood pressure, but radical stances don't have a big enough impact on educational institutions to change kids' chances of success.

As a radical centrist in education, I subscribe to the following principles:

1. Adopt an "and" not "or" mind-set.
2. Look for truth and value in all beliefs and practices.
3. Respect the perspective of the individual.
4. Recognize that one size does not fit all (kids or teachers).
5. Attend to attitudes.
6. Understand that the elephant can only be eaten one bite at a time.
7. Make sure everyone is moving forward, not just the early adopters.
8. Don't be afraid to say, "I don't know."
9. Believe that measurement is good, but not everything can be measured.
10. Know and keep your core values.

Let me explain . . .

ADOPT AN "AND" NOT "OR" MIND-SET

> *The answer to most multiple-choice questions is Yes.*
>
> —*Walt Crawford, 2004, p. 64*

Believe it or not, there are a lot of people with very strongly held opinions. I'm always reading or hearing a good deal of either-or type thinking.

- Separate or integrated technology curriculum
- *Encyclopaedia Britannica* or Wikipedia
- Evolutionary or revolutionary educational change
- Content knowledge or process skills
- Testing or assessment
- Set curriculum or teacher choice

- Print or online resources
- Face-to-face or online classes

It's this sort of black-and-white thinking that makes for stimulating reading and engenders reader outpourings of love or hate.

I'd encourage you, however, to go back and read an old column by Walt Crawford, "The Dangers of Uniformity," that appeared in the September 2004 issue of *American Libraries*. In it he writes: "Why do so many of us look for single solutions to current problems, single technologies, single media? Why do so many writers, futurists, and speakers tout X as 'the future' rather than 'a part of the future'? I've used the slogan 'And, not Or' for more than a decade. There's another slogan that goes along with it, one that I believe to be at least partly true in most walks of life: 'The answer to most multiple-choice questions is Yes'" (p. 64). Walt's philosophy is one worth adopting. Next time you are asked if something should be x or y, try to answer, "Yes, x *and* y."

LOOK FOR TRUTH AND VALUE IN ALL BELIEFS AND PRACTICES

If you can't stand someone because they can't tolerate others, does that make you hypocritical? If so, should you tolerate their intolerance?

—*Anonymous*

I find following my own advice here is tough—really tough. My first reaction to people with whom I disagree is to consider them idiots and want to dope slap them. Not a course of action approved, I'm sure, by the late Mother Teresa.

What is difficult to reconcile is that those people I think need to be slapped usually aren't dopes at all. In fact, more than a few are a lot smarter than I am. How does one account for a situation in which two intelligent people disagree? Well . . .

- One or both could be uninformed about the topic at hand.
- One or both could be misinformed about the topic at hand.
- But, most likely, those in disagreement bring different values or perspectives to the topic, thus giving specific facts, experiences, or arguments more or less weight. Looking at it this way, *all* evidence ought to be seen as having potential value.

It is dangerous to mistake disagreement for stupidity, or even ignorance. We must listen, learn, and at times moderate our own views if we are to retain the Radical Center of Education. In order to find areas of mutual agreement, one needs to keep climbing the abstraction ladder until both parties find a common goal, even if there never is a consensus on the steps needed to reach the goal. (Why, yes, we both want to improve the world. There's something we have in common!)

A related mind-set I find difficult not to adopt is assuming a hidden agenda or unstated ulterior motive on another's part. Yes, I certainly do think that those who advocate for school vouchers are actually advocating for the demise of public education, but one can only effectively argue with *stated goals,* not those we ascribe to others.

Two "sides," each stubbornly and blindly adhering to a single tenet, will not result in change. When both sides move to the Radical Center, based on finding mutual values, change is more likely to happen.

RESPECT THE PERSPECTIVE OF THE INDIVIDUAL

Miles's Law: Where you stand depends on where you sit.

One of the benefits (or curses) of serving on a school's districtwide committees is learning about the challenges and goals of a variety of employees—classroom teachers, students, principals, librarians, technicians, maintenance staff, clerks, and paraprofessionals. A number of school committees have parents and other citizens as members. What we too often call "turf battles" are actually issues viewed from individual and specific group vantage points—different "frames" to problems. What makes this interesting is that goodwilled individuals can have widely differing perspectives.

Budgeting is one area in which this is radically apparent. The question of whether more dollars are best spent on technology, lower class sizes, or tuck-pointing brick walls will be answered, legitimately, honestly, and differently, depending on whether it is the technology director, a social studies teacher with classes of forty students, or the head of maintenance answering the question.

The issues of digital copyright protection may look very different depending on whether one is a producer or consumer of the creative product. One's definition of "adequate" network security will depend on whether one is a technician whose life will be made miserable by a virus or a classroom teacher who finds multiple log-in screens time consuming and frustrating. The description of "appropriate" Internet content certainly depends on one's personal values.

If change is going to happen, the voices of all stakeholders need to be heard. Different doesn't mean right or wrong. It just means different. Empathy is an increasingly important skill. If I could take steroids for any leadership strength, this is where I would like to bulk up.

RECOGNIZE THAT ONE SIZE DOES NOT FIT ALL (KIDS OR TEACHERS)

Always remember that you are unique. Just like everybody else.

The goal most requested by parents from our district's 1998 strategic planning was an individual education plan for every student, not just those identified as having special needs. How interesting that parents, *even more than we educators,* recognize each child as an individual.

Ecologists talk about the advantages of biodiversity—a wide variety of living things that create a healthier biome. Why do we not talk more about edu-diversity in our classrooms? (And about how differentiated instruction means more than just different reading levels of materials?) Too often when the next great thing (constructivism, technology, whole-language reading instruction, integrated math, data-driven decision making, professional learning communities, and so on) comes along, it is considered a silver bullet and other methods and philosophies are denigrated and pushed aside. We need to regard the "next great thing" as *another* tool in a big educational utility belt, not the only one of value.

There is no educational strategy (unless it involves some sort of cruelty) that does not work for at least some people under some circumstances. And there is no educational strategy that works with every person every time. An educational monoculture is no healthier than a suburban lawn.

The "one size does not fit all" principle is something we technology users might keep in mind more often when we get enthusiastic about a particular tool or service and then are disappointed when other teachers yawn or even ignore us. Try as I might, I simply don't "get" why people love cell phones, yet other folks seem to rely on them heavily. I suppose if I expect you to respect my taste in this matter, it behooves me to respect yours as well.

This is why the "and" not "or" mind-set is so important. Our educational system needs to be as diverse as the kids and teachers in it.

ATTEND TO ATTITUDES

If you think you can do a thing or think you can't do a thing, you're right.

—Henry Ford

Those of us who wish to honor the Radical Center of Education need to remember the critical role attitude plays in change efforts—especially those involving technology. If we set about determining whether we in education are using tech tools well, we need to ask about attitude as well as skills.

I find it amazing (and even a little frustrating) that some teachers can't get enough technology in their classrooms and can't give their kids enough experiences using it, whereas other teachers still grumble at even having to use anything more complicated than an overhead projector. And the division doesn't break down neatly along generational lines either.

If you want to encourage more constructive use of technology in your school, the following strategies can help shape your attitudes and those of your fellow teachers:

- When introducing a new technology, stress the WIIFM (What's In It For Me) reasons for its use. Any new project should have at its heart the clear goal of making a task easier or providing the kind of exciting learning opportunities that make teaching more enjoyable.

- Give end users a voice in deciding equipment platforms, the software adopted, and timelines for implementation. Everyone hates top-down edicts.

- Take a hard look at training times to make sure they are as convenient as possible for everyone. Consider a range of training options that suit individual teacher learning styles. Although many people learn well in hands-on, face-to-face training sessions, others may prefer online or video instruction, well-written tutorials, or simply the time and peace needed to learn through experimentation.

- Attend to our own attitudes when working with others. When we help other teachers with computer hardware and usage problems, are we doing our best in making sure they are respected for the intelligent, loveable people they really are? And do we insist on some respect when we ourselves are taught? We should.

Never underestimate the power of attitude.

UNDERSTAND THAT THE ELEPHANT CAN ONLY BE EATEN ONE BITE AT A TIME

Mrs. Weiler's Law: Anything is edible if it is chopped finely enough.

As much as they may be needed, radical changes in education are less likely than incremental changes. Despite Disraeli's often-quoted caveat, "The most dangerous strategy is to jump a chasm in two leaps," stepping too far outside a teacher's or administrator's comfort zone means leaving the Radical Center of Education and makes long-term, universal change more difficult. And the larger the leap expected to be made in a single bound, the fewer who are willing to take the chance. And nobody can *force* anybody to do anything in education.

The more analogous a technology application is to something the teacher is already doing, the more likely the teacher is to adopt it. Mobile laptop carts—not too popular; interactive whiteboards—hugely successful.

Vygotsky's proximal development theory holds for adult learners as well as for kids: you've always got to have some old knowledge from which to hang the new learning. Chasm leaping doesn't allow for this; bite-size elephant eating does. Never apologize for taking an incremental approach to technology implementation in the classroom. This approach gets teachers actually using the technology to improve the classroom experience, even if it isn't radically overhauling it.

As much as I might wish it were otherwise, technology is not really a catalyst for change but simply a tool for change. It can be an effective and exciting way to help implement best practices driven by content-area research, educational theory, or even state and national mandates, but change shouldn't start with technology.

MAKE SURE EVERYONE IS MOVING FORWARD, NOT JUST THE EARLY ADOPTERS

> *To travel fast, travel alone. To travel far, travel with others.*
>
> —*African proverb*

I thought of this saying after a blog post caught my eye. A tech director recently wrote that . . .

- Checking e-mail
- Searching the Internet
- Playing Internet-based games
- Word processing
- Using Excel spreadsheets

. . . struck him as outdated. *His* computer use consists of social networking, using wikis, editing and sharing photos online, and listening to streaming audio, as well as "crafting video-intensive presentations."

Most of the activities on this technologist's list would make my list too, as well as the lists of many technology enthusiasts. Yet a 2007 survey shows that 73 percent of Americans have "never heard of" Google Docs (Linder, 2007). I wonder what percentage of Americans have heard of the other applications this technologist uses? What's the percentage of teachers who use social networking sites professionally? I'll bet dollars to doughnuts it wouldn't even be close to 73 percent.

Speeding ahead is easy to do for those of us interested and invested in technology. But if experience has taught me anything, a school district needs to measure its technological achievements by how the *majority* of its teachers are using technology, not by the practices of its few shining stars—its "pockets of wow."

The Radical Center emphasizes smaller, deeper, more widespread, and lasting change through the use of technology. The problem with being too far down the road ahead of the pack is turning around to find that everyone else has taken a different path.

DON'T BE AFRAID TO SAY, "I DON'T KNOW"

Discussion is an exchange of knowledge; argument is an exchange of ignorance.

—*Robert Quillen*

It's difficult to admit, but there are darned few things I know for absolutely certain, especially when it comes to technology and education. Thankfully, the older I get, the easier it is for me to say, "I don't know, but let's find out." Try it a couple times. It gets easier.

For some reason, our culture has replaced evidence with volume on too many issues. Although it's easy to say to those with whom one does not agree that they lack supporting evidence for their position, the Radical Center of Education believes one needs to critically view the amount and validity of both (or all) perspectives. Self-examination of one's own beliefs is necessary for credibility. And to come to consensus on controversial issues, a consensus that vital information is missing (or is unknowable) must be reached.

We have to change the culture of our schools so that asking questions is considered a sign of wisdom, not weakness.

Oh, and it is perfectly reasonable to conclude at times that "the verdict is still out." Conclusive evidence is not always available.

BELIEVE THAT MEASUREMENT IS GOOD, BUT NOT EVERYTHING CAN BE MEASURED

Not everything that counts can be counted. And not everything that can be counted counts.

—*Albert Einstein*

Donald Norman, in his terrific book *Things That Make Us Smart* (1994, p. 15), said it well:

> Technology aids our thoughts and civilized lives, but it also provides a mind-set that artificially elevates some aspects of life and ignores others, not based upon their real importance but rather by the arbitrary condition of whether they can be measured scientifically and objectively by today's tools. Consequently, science and technology tend to deal solely with the products of their measurements, they divorce themselves from the real world. The danger is that things that cannot be measured play no role in scientific work and are judged to be of little importance. Science and technology do what they can do

and ignore the rest. They are superb at what they do, but what is left out can be of equal or greater importance.

We're certainly focused on "empirical evidence" and "evidence-based practice" and testing, testing, testing in education lately. We're devoting tremendous resources (including technology and technology staff) to online testing, value-added testing, data warehousing, and data analysis. Perhaps we are overdue in public education for such an accounting. Unfortunately, that which we can measure given the limits of current testing is a small subset of those attributes that make people successful. This has led to discounting those programs and activities that do not show a direct bearing on basic, low-level test scores.

Data are good. No question. (I look for numbers that support my point of view all the time.) But we in the Radical Center of Education must remember that "what is left out can be of equal or greater importance" and acknowledge values other than empirical evidence if positive change is to occur. We ought to be giving equal credence to professional experience; anecdotal information; meaningful traditions; and the intrinsic value of such activities and programs as play, sports, the arts, libraries, and storytelling.

The Radical Center of Education honors multiple kinds of evidence, not just data (or just anecdotes, or just tradition, and so on), and uses them to direct and make change.

KNOW AND KEEP YOUR CORE VALUES

> *You've got to stand for something or you'll fall for anything.*

The Radical Center of Education theory doesn't work unless the person working for change has deeply held values. Although Stephen Colbert makes great sport of the know-nothing philosophy of "truthiness," making Radical Center change requires an open mind as well as values firmly held by both the heart and the head. Without such values, change is simply change for change's sake.

I can't recommend a single source of these values, nor should I expect anyone to adopt mine. I will list a few of my own and encourage you to create your own list.

- The solution to most of the world's problems will rely on effective education.
- My best judgments are made when I think of myself first as a child advocate, second as an educator, and last as a technologist.
- All kids should be treated the way I want my own grandchildren to be treated.
- Creativity, empathy, and humor are as important to success as reading, writing, and numeracy.
- Schools should teach children to think, not to believe.

Your list will be as individual as you are. But know it and act with it in mind.

The author of *The Purpose Driven Life,* Rick Warren, and his wife, Kay, were being interviewed on National Public Radio's *Speaking of Faith* program. As a couple, they lead a large evangelical church, but they also are working on AIDS prevention. One particular comment by Kay stuck with me. She sees her church as a moderate organization, neither fundamentalist nor liberal. And she believes this to be the most difficult position for it to take because it has two sets of critics—those from both the extreme left and the extreme right. Anyone who chooses the Radical Center can count on doubling his or her critics. Be warned.

Change is tough—especially meaningful, lasting, and humane change. The Radical Center might be a way to help it actually come about.

The Giant and the Ants: How Problems Are Solved

A tour guide in Nairobi, Kenya, told me this pourquoi story about how the Ngong (Knuckle) Hills just outside the city came into being.

A giant once ravished the surrounding land. The animals of the savanna were determined to be rid of it. The big animals went in first: the elephants, the rhinos, the lions. Each in turn were soundly trounced by the giant.

That night all the ants gathered and decided each would carry a few clumps of dirt and place them on the giant while he was asleep. They reasoned that they made up for their lack of size by their sheer numbers.

By the next morning the giant was buried so deep that he never rose again. All that can be seen today are the protruding knuckles of one hand—the Ngong Hills.

As teachers, sometimes we feel that we cannot make a difference in solving "giant" problems in education. But I would encourage you carefully to consider who in the long run can make the most improvements in education: politicians, departments of education, consultants, administrators—or every teacher making some small changes every year?

I hope this book has provided you with the guidance and inspiration to make a few changes with technology starting tomorrow in your classroom. You will be making a bigger difference than you might realize.

Readings and Resources

As a practical guide, this book does not go deeply into the research, philosophy, or visions of educational technology use. But over the past twenty years a good deal has been written about the impact of technology on society and education. And new writings, and increasingly videos, appear every day. What follows is a somewhat eclectic list of resources that I have found to be consistently clarifying and challenging. They are roughly grouped by the book chapters to which they are most closely aligned.

I have purposely chosen not to include Internet links to online resources in this book. The fluid nature of the Internet makes such links quickly outdated, and most of the resources mentioned in this book are usually just a Google search away. Contact me personally if you have any problems locating any materials.

Chapter One: Why Should Classroom Teachers Be Technologically Skillful?

ASSOCIATIONS

The International Society for Technology in Education (ISTE) is the leading professional organization devoted to educational technology use. It does have an international scope and has a broad spectrum of educators as members: technologists, classroom teachers, college professors, librarians, and educational technology company representatives. It holds an annual conference each year near the end of June at a variety of U.S. locations. *Learning & Leading with Technology,* its primary journal, is published eight times a year. The organization is well known for its NETS technology standards for students, teachers, and administrators. ISTE has several special interest groups (SIGs) devoted to members of individual job types or to those with interests in specific uses of technology.

The American Association of School Librarians is a division of the American Library Association. Its membership comprises primarily school library media specialists and library school professors. A strong technology strand is a part of its biannual conference, and its publication *Knowledge Quest* often deals with technology-related issues—especially information literacy, intellectual freedom, and safe and responsible Internet use.

The Partnership for 21st Century Skills has been an influential player in promoting technology use in education. Made up primarily of companies with an interest in education and technology, its Framework for 21st Century Learning is well respected.

SOME INFLUENTIAL WRITERS IN THE FIELD

Here are a (very) few of the major writers and thinkers (some of whom do both!) in the field of educational technology, along with some of their major works.

Anne Collier. The NetFamilyNews blog; the Web site ConnectSafely; and the free booklet *A Parents' Guide to Facebook*, ConnectSafely, 2010 (with Larry Magid).

Ian Jukes. The Committed Sardine blog and the book *Understanding the Digital Generation: Teaching and Learning in the New Digital Landscape*, Thousand Oaks, Calif.: Corwin Press, 2010 (with Ted McCain and Lee Crockett).

Jamie McKenzie. The *From Now On* journal and the book *Beyond Cut-and-Paste*, Bellingham, Wash.: FNO Press, 2009.

Alan November. The book *Empowering Students with Technology*, Thousand Oaks, Calif.: Corwin Press, 2009. (Alan's Building Learning Communities annual conference is highly regarded.)

Will Richardson. The Weblogg-Ed blog and the book *Blogs, Wikis, Podcasts, and Other Powerful Web Tools for Classrooms* (3rd ed.), Thousand Oaks, Calif.: Corwin Press, 2010.

David Warlick. The 2¢ Worth blog and the book *Redefining Literacy 2.0*, Santa Barbara, Calif.: Linworth Books, 2008.

TECHNOLOGY CRITICS AND SKEPTICS

A healthy dose of skepticism about any endeavor in which large amounts of money are involved is a very good thing. These publications are thoughtful reading for all educators.

Alliance for Childhood. *Fool's Gold* (2000) and *Tech Tonic* (2004) reports.

Baurlein, Mark. *The Dumbest Generation: How the Digital Age Stupefies Young Americans and Jeopardizes Our Future (or, Don't Trust Anyone Under 30)*. New York: Tarcher, 2009.

Carr, Nicholas. *The Shallows: What the Internet is Doing to Our Brains*. New York: Norton, 2010.

Cuban, Larry. *Oversold and Underused: Computers in the Classroom*. Cambridge, Mass.: Harvard University Press, 2003.

Healey, Jane. *Failure to Connect: How Computers Affect Our Children's Minds—and What We Can Do About It*. New York: Simon & Schuster, 1999.

OTHER EDUCATION AND TECHNOLOGY THINKERS

Costa, Art. *Learning and Leading with Habits of Mind*. Alexandria, Va.: ASCD, 2008.

Kurzweil, Ray. *The Age of Spiritual Machines: When Computers Exceed Human Intelligence*. New York: Penguin, 2000.

Maiers, Angela, and Amy Sanford. *The Passion-Driven Classroom: A Framework for Teaching and Learning*. Larchmont, N.Y.: Eye on Education, 2010.

Moore, Geoffrey. *Inside the Tornado: Strategies for Developing, Leveraging, and Surviving Hypergrowth Markets*. New York: Harper, 2004.

Pink, Daniel. *Drive: The Surprising Truth About What Motivates Us*. New York: Riverhead, 2010.

Robinson, Sir Ken. *The Element: How Finding Your Passion Changes Everything*. New York: Penguin, 2009.

Zuboff, Shoshana. *In the Age of the Smart Machine*. New York: Basic Books, 1989.

Chapter Two: Q&A About Some Basics

Ereben, Cara. "Cloud Computing: The Economic Imperative." *ESchool News*, March 4, 2009.

Kaplan, Jeffrey. "Five Myths About SaaS." CIO.com, March 23, 2009.

"Security & Privacy." Google Apps for Education, n.d.

Williamson, Marianne. *A Return to Love: Reflections on the Principles of a Course in Miracles*. New York: HarperCollins, 1996.

Chapter Three: Using Technology for Professional Productivity

"NETS for Teachers." International Society for Technology in Education, 2008.

Chapter Five: Teaching 21st-Century Skills

American Library Association. *Information Literacy Standards for Student Learning*. Chicago: American Library Association, 1998.

Breen, Bill. "The 6 Myths of Creativity." Fastcompany.com, Dec. 1, 2004.

Duncan, Donna, and Laura Lockhart. *I-Search, You Search, We All Learn to Research*. New York: Neal-Schuman, 2000.

Eisenberg, Michael, Doug Johnson, and Robert Berkowitz. "Information, Communications, and Technology (ICT) Skills Curriculum Based on the Big6 Skills Approach to Information Problem-Solving." *Library Media Connection*, May-June 2010, 28(6), 24–29.

Friedman, Thomas. *The World Is Flat: A Brief History of the Twenty-first Century*. New York: Farrar, Straus and Giroux, 2005.

Johnson, Mary. *Primary Sources in the Library: A Collaboration Guide for Library Media Specialists*. Santa Barbara, Calif.: Linworth Books, 2003.

Macrorie, Ken. *The I-Search Paper: Revised Edition of Searching Writing*. Portsmouth, N.H.: Boynton/Cook, 1998.

Pink, Daniel. *A Whole New Mind: Moving from the Information Age to the Conceptual Age*. New York: Riverhead, 2006.

Chapter Six: Managing Disruptive Technologies in the Classroom

Christensen, Clayton, Curtis W. Johnson, and Michael B. Horn. *Disrupting Class: How Disruptive Innovation Will Change the Way the World Learns*. New York: McGraw-Hill, 2008.

Lindsay, Julie, and Vicki Davis. Flat Classroom® Project (Web site).

Prensky, Marc. "In Educational Games COMPLEXITY MATTERS—Mini-Games are Trivial—but 'Complex' Games Are Not." Marc Prensky (Web site), 2005.

Chapter Seven: Commonsense Practices for Safe and Ethical Technology Use

Center for Social Media. *Code of Best Practices in Fair Use for Media Literacy*. Washington DC: School of Communication at American University, 2009.

Hegna, Jen, and Doug Johnson. "Guidelines for Teachers Using Social and Educational Networks." *Library Media Connection*, Mar.-Apr. 2010, 28(5), 50–53.

Jenkins, Henry. *Confronting the Challenges of Participatory Culture*. MacArthur Foundation, Chicago, Il, 2006.

Johnson, Doug. *Connections for Learning: Schools and the Educational Use of Social Networking*. Fountain Hills, Ariz.: Saywire, 2009.

Magid, Larry, and Anne Collier, "Predators and Cyberbullies: Reality Check." ConnectSafely, 2007.

"Statistics." National Center for Missing & Exploited Children, 2011.

Willard, Nancy. *Educator's Guide to Cyberbullying and Cyberthreats*. Eugene, Oreg.: Center for Safe and Responsible Use of the Internet, 2007.

Chapter Eight: Developing a Long-Term Learning Strategy

Valenza, Joyce, and Doug Johnson. "Reboot Camp." *School Library Journal*, May 2008, 54(5), 56–57.

Warlick, David. *A Gardener's Approach to Learning*. Raleigh, N.C.: The Landmark Project, 2010.

Chapter Nine: Looking into the Crystal Ball

Crawford, Walt. "The Dangers of Uniformity." *American Libraries*, September 2004, 63(10), 64.

Cuban, Larry. *How Can I Fix It? Finding Solutions and Managing Dilemmas*. New York: Teachers College Press, 2001.

Linder, Brad. "Study: 73% of Americans Have Never Heard of Google Docs." DownloadSquad, December 17, 2007.

New Media Consortium. *The Horizon Report*, 2004 through 2011 (annual).

New Media Consortium. *The Horizon Report: K–12 Edition*, 2009 through 2011 (annual).

Norman, Donald. *Things That Make Us Smart: Defending Human Attributes in the Age of the Machine*. New York: Basic Books, 1994.

Tippett, Krista. "The New Evangelical Leaders Part II: Rick and Kay Warren." *Speaking of Faith* (American Public Media), December 6, 2007.

Index